America's Oil Wars

America's Oil Wars

Stephen Pelletière

PRAEGER

Westport, Connecticut
London

Library of Congress Cataloging-in-Publication Data

Pelletière, Stephen C.
America's oil wars / Stephen C. Pelletière.
p. cm.
Includes bibliographical references and index.
ISBN 0-275-97851-6 (alk. paper)
1. Iraq War, 2003—Causes. 2. Iraq War, 2003—Moral and ethical aspects—United States. 3. Petroleum industry and trade—Political aspects—United States. 4. Petroleum industry and trade—Political aspects—Iraq. I. Title.
DS79.76.P35 2004
956.7044′3—dc22   2004040077

British Library Cataloguing in Publication Data is available.

Library of Congress Catalog Card Number: 2004040077
ISBN: 0-275-97851-6

First published in 2004

Praeger Publishers, 88 Post Road West, Westport, CT 06881
An imprint of Greenwood Publishing Group, Inc.
www.praeger.com

Printed in the United States of America

The paper used in this book complies with the
Permanent Paper Standard issued by the National
Information Standards Organization (Z39.48-1984).

10 9 8 7 6 5 4 3 2 1

To Jean

War's a racket.
—Smedley Butler, America's most decorated general

Contents

Introduction

This book attempts to explain why the United States invaded and occupied Iraq. It seeks to discover a rationale for the Bush administration's action, one that is adequate to encompass the enormity of what was done. The action that Bush took was awful: he led America to war under false pretenses. The claims he made—about Saddam having weapons of mass destruction and his having links to al Qaeda—were not true.

What was it that was so important about invading and occupying Iraq that Bush would have been driven to such lengths?

The answer that we are going to give is that he feared a significant imbalance of power, not just in the Persian Gulf but worldwide. And this potential imbalance arose out of the outcome of the Iran-Iraq War, where the Iraqis unexpectedly, and decisively, defeated the Iranians after a hard-fought eight-year conflict.

Saddam Hussein stood at a crossroads then. He had a million men under arms, he had a general staff that had proven itself competent by subduing the Iranians, and he had a window of opportunity in which to maneuver in order to make himself the leader of the Arab world.

But Saddam's gaze was fixed on a much more substantial prize—he wanted to control the Organization of Petroleum Exporting Countries (OPEC) and turn it into a bona fide cartel. Had he been able to do that, he would have gained immensely. A well-disciplined OPEC, where all of the members were solidaric, could have exercised enormous international influence. The individual who was able to marshal the resources of so great (and powerful) an institution, and keep its members in line, would have been someone with whom to reckon.

The United States was not about to see Saddam fill that role, and so, as this study will show, it began to cut him down to size, starting with the first Gulf War in 1991 and ending with war number two against Iraq (in 2003), where it effectively finished him off.

The book establishes that this was what drove the Americans. But it also carries the analysis further. It examines the morality of Saddam's action in trying to get control of OPEC and advance his country to the front rank of nations.

It concludes that the case is not so clearcut against Saddam as the Bush administration has tried to make out. Saddam had a lot of morality on his side, not as the leader of an isolated nation-state but as a member of a broader constituency of resource-rich (but poor) southern tier countries trying to make their way in the world.

The book is divided into five chapters. The first explores the context of events that produced 9/11, the pretext Bush used to ensnare Saddam in a trap from which the Iraqi could not extricate himself.

It looks at the nature of the so-called Islamic Fundamentalist movement with which Saddam supposedly was involved. The book concludes that not only was he not conspiring with the Fundamentalists, there was no such movement at all. This book contends that Western analysts have gotten it wrong about Fundamentalism.

By putting forth a simple, coherent explanation of why the Twin Towers disaster occurred (one that has nothing to do with aggressive terror), the book sets the stage for an examination of America's motives for thrusting itself into a part of the world that, because of the religious sensibilities of Muslims, ought never to have been trespassed upon.

In chapter 2 we introduce the topic of oil, which is what originally drew the Americans to the Gulf. We discuss the idea of an oil system to control production so as to influence price, the only way the industry could be made profitable. We discuss how the Great Cartel gained such control and exercised it till the 1973 OPEC Revolution.

Chapter 3 describes the breakdown of the system the oilmen imposed. The solvent that ate away at it—and ultimately brought it down—was nationalism, and the two foremost nationalists with which we deal are the Shah of Iran and Saddam Hussein. We also take up the introduction of arms-trading activities on a monumental scale into the Persian Gulf.

In chapter 4 we deal with the first war of the United States against Iraq, a brutal affair. We examine what it was that induced the Americans to devastate what, relatively speaking, was a defenseless country. We introduce the neo-conservatives, who largely were responsible for crafting America's strategy toward Iraq.

In chapter 5 we look at the Afghan war that, we claim, was America's Spanish Civil War, where it tried out tactics and weapons with the aim of developing a style of warfare that would make the United States invincible.

We show why this latter-day blitzkrieg approach has not worked out for Washington, and then we go on to consider the claims of the oil producers against the consuming states. We believe the course that the United States has embarked on (of seizing the assets it feels it must have) is extraordinarily shortsighted. Without morality on its side, it is unlikely that, in the long term, Americans will be able to fulfill their agenda.

CHAPTER 1

The Origins of Religious Unrest in the Middle East in the 1990s

Starting in 1990, a series of incidents occurred in the Middle East that seemed to presage a movement of Islamic revivalism. In Algeria, Fundamentalists captured a number of seats in the local elections, embarrassing the government party that, until then, had enjoyed virtually unchallenged authority.[1] Quickly afterward in Jordan, the king, to propitiate a public maddened by food rioting, agreed to hold elections, in which religious parties participated and achieved considerable success.[2] Next the Tunisians uncovered what they claimed was a plot to overthrow the regime there: caches of weapons, presumably belonging to Muslim terrorists, were put on display in Tunis.[3] In Egypt, almost coincidentally, an incident occurred in one of the poorer neighborhoods of Cairo where a Muslim stabbed a Coptic Christian, and afterward a Muslim mob set the neighborhood afire.[4]

Outside the Arab world, Muslims seemed to bestir themselves. In the Trans-Caucases, Azerbaijani Shias attacked Armenian Christians, killing a number and driving others into exile. Later, Azerbaijan joined fellow Soviet republics in declaring independence.[5] Several of the breakaways, according to Russian analysts, could now be expected to form an "Islamic union."

This increase in Islamic action raised fears of a grand upheaval by over a billion Muslims, not merely in the Middle East but throughout the world. Indeed, it was claimed at the time that the world was witnessing a second wave of Khomeiniism, a new *jihad*, one emanating from Arab lands (the original Khomeiniism, deriving from Iran, was non-Arab).

Despite all of the sensationalizing in the media, however, the revival, as of the early 1990s, was really too vague to characterize. Moreover, reports received were vexingly contradictory. There were, for example, persistent claims of huge cash flows from the Persian Gulf to Islamist groups, across the Magreb mainly.[6] The money supposedly was coming from wealthy sheikhs expressly seeking to undermine the rule of secularists like Egypt's Hosni Mubarak.

At the same time, however, other apparently knowledgeable sources questioned the sense of such allegations, since the sheikhs who were being singled out for mention were extremely conservative, not to say reactionary. They were individuals who would never promote mass protest, any form of popular unrest being anathema to them.[7]

As of the early 1990s, all that one could say was that the area clearly was undergoing some sort of transformation and that the nature of the unrest was decidedly religious. But what was causing the upset and why it was spreading so widely were questions for which no one seemed to have answers. Eventually, the line that America would take toward the phenomenon would be influential, as would be the response of the secular Arab governments.

Most influential, however, as this book will argue, was the world economic situation, because at the center of all the violence were a lot of youths. Wherever Muslim effervescence appeared, invariably there were unemployed youths mixed up in it.

In looking into how the so-called movement of Islamic Fundamentalism grew up, we pursue three lines of attack. First, we give an overview of activity in the three most affected areas: Algeria, Egypt, and the Levant (Israel and the Occupied Territories). Then we venture some observations on the nature of the events described, and then we give our revisionist view of what this was all about. After that we discuss the efforts of the administration of George W. Bush to tie Islamic Fundamentalism to what the administration claimed was an anti-Western jihad.

By treating the outbreaks separately and by putting the discussion into a regional context, we seek to counter the tendency, marked whenever Fundamentalism is discussed, of treating it as a globe-girdling movement. Movements (as we construe them) have to be able to mobilize masses of adherents in the streets. Islamic Fundamentalism nowhere had that capability. Individual groupings—which later on it was claimed were part of the putative Islamic Fundamentalist movement—did have the ability, but what was essential (and what was never done) was to show that the groups, located all over the world, were carrying on a conspiracy directed by a central controlling unit, one that could orchestrate continent-wide upheavals.

We begin with the rise of the Islamic Salvation Front (FIS; *Front Islamique du Salut*) in Algeria, the party that, practically in-and-of-itself, drew the world's attention to Fundamentalism.

The Algeria Experience

The sharp fall in oil prices that undercut the economies of the Arab countries in the mid-1980s showed the ineptitude of many of the Middle East's *dirigiste* regimes, like Algeria's National Liberation Front (NLF; *Front de Liberation Nationale*).[8]

With the oil price collapse, the dirigiste regimes lost out financially. Algeria was particularly hard hit as it practically lived off oil.[9] Whereas in the past the regime had responded to crises by, in effect, throwing money at them, now, in a cash-strapped environment, it could not, it appeared, even begin to cope.

A related trauma for the dirigiste regimes was the collapse of the Soviet Union, and this was because many of the Arab Socialist governments were clients of the Soviets. It was a kind of one–two punch that hit the Arab Socialists at this time.

Algeria is a classic example of how one such regime stumbled when bad times struck. The unexpected discomfiture of the party politicians opened up opportunities for traditionalist forces, which had been, from the ouster of the French in 1962, more or less suppressed.

Thirty years after its emergence as an independent state, Algeria suffered from a kind of national sclerosis; elite circulation was stalled. The elite that took over the rule after the ouster yet held on to power, its ranks comprising descendents of so-called martyrs who struggled in the original 1962 revolt. This lot was estimated in the early 1990s to be about 600,000 families.

In a society of some 32 million, this was a significant percentage. Moreover, not only was this privileged class grandfathered into the power structure, as it were, it had numerous cultural advantages as well. Chief among them was the fact of its being francophone (and francophile). The bureaucracy conducted its business in French. The very best people aped the latest French fashions; they vacationed in France; they sent their children to school there.

As for the masses, they were the Arabic speakers (or else Berber, the significant minority group). Effectively, Algerian society was riven, top to bottom. Anyone of the lower classes who aimed to gain a place in it had first to transform himself: he had, in a manner of speaking, to become a pretend-Frenchmen.

The instrument whereby privileges were distributed to the elite was the FLN. A vanguard party, the FLN had by the 1990s ceased to concern itself overmuch with mass mobilization; its leaders felt, evidently, that they had a mandate to lead.

As long as Algeria had cash, this heedless style of rule could be practiced. At the same time, however, in the late 1980s it was estimated unemployment in Algeria was over 30 percent. That figure comprised mainly youths, since over 70 percent of the country was less than thirty years old. The government dole enabled the youngsters to get by.

The dole could not solve everything, however. Some problems, like housing, were veritable running sores. Shortages of living space particularly affected the youth, and more specifically the so-called *baladi* youth, rustics who had immigrated to the major cities from the countryside.[10]

Because apartments were unavailable—and those few that did come on to the market went to the *privilegeurs*—the housing situation was a constant irritant. If a young man could not obtain living quarters (away from his family, that is), he could not marry, and, in a sternly Muslim country, that meant that he could not have a productive personal life.

Thus, when, in the mid-1980s, money began to be in tight supply, the youths, who already were chaffing under societally imposed constraints, found themselves constrained further by the new austerity. The "reforms" were, to a large degree, driven by the International Monetary Fund (IMF), to which the government had applied for assistance.[11]

Unfortunately for the FLN leadership, this already tense situation became further charged when, in the midst of a particularly hot summer, the capital's water supply system broke down. Algiers erupted in rioting, the mobs comprising these same disaffected youths who now rampaged through the city for several days.

In desperation, the government called out the army, which botched the pacification effort and ended up killing perhaps 200 civilians, both rioters and, one assumes, noninvolved lookers-on.[12]

This threw the government into greater disarray. In an attempt to recoup, it promulgated a program of political reforms, including the opening up of the electoral process. Parties other than the FLN would be permitted to compete at the polls. This was a real transformation, one the government evidently believed it could manage. It seems to have believed that the new parties would cancel each other out, since the newcomers would have to develop constituencies, which would take time, and consequently no clear challenger to the FLN would emerge.

The FLN overlooked one thing: one element in the community—the religious—was set to go, so to speak. When the government decision to hold elections came, the religious was already well positioned to compete.

The Free Mosque Network

We mentioned previously that Algeria's youth were discommoded as long as the housing shortage persisted. They were forced to live with their parents, and because Algerian families are large (and apartments small), sleeping arrangements were well-nigh impossible. Youths were forced to sleep in shifts. Algiers was a town where, after midnight, legions of youth prowled the city, effectively taking their turn on the streets while siblings used the family beds.

Throughout Algiers an element of the religious community had set up makeshift neighborhood mosques, which were accessible at all hours. The night-prowling youth could drop in at any time, get a bowl of soup, warm themselves in winter, and pass the hours in desultory conversation with whomever happened to be hanging out, so to speak.

According to intelligence sources, these so-called free mosques became centers of antigovernment activity.[13] The talk there was about government shortcomings. Attempts were made by the imams who maintained the mosques to induce those who dropped by to speak out on such matters.

People who did not understand the setup in Algeria speculated after the fact (after the FLN's disastrous showing at the polls) that the *whole* religious community in Algeria had turned against the government and that the opposition was mobilized through these free mosques. Actually, the situation was more complicated than that.

In Algeria (as is the case with many Arab countries), the government routinely subsidizes the clerical establishment. In return, the official clergy (as they are known) are expected to follow the government's line on important issues. During the disturbances of the early 1990s, the official clergy did support the government. Not so with the imams of the free mosques, who were receiving private subsidization and therefore were not beholden to the government. Allegedly, these imams were the troublemakers.

The money for the privately subsidized mosques came from out of the country. Most of the funds came mainly from the Gulf, passing through the hands of local (Algerian) agents, who regularly would travel out to the Gulf where they would importune the rich sheikhs.

It was later reckoned (after the FLN had received its serious setback at the polls) that these free mosques had been converted to get-out-the-vote institutions for the new religious party, the FIS. When the votes for the first round of elections were tallied, it was seen that the FIS had scored a great upset. The religious took 40 percent of the mayoralities.[14]

The FLN had the option, then, of cancelling the next round of voting. Instead, it announced that the poll would go ahead; however the FLN tried to rig the result through gerrymandering. At that, rioting reerupted; the army had to be called back out on to the streets, more casualties ensued, and the government ended up rescinding the gerrymandering, after which the elections went on. This time the FIS won 149 of the 430 seats in the Assembly, a clear plurality. This led the army to intervene. It cancelled the result, and the civilians who had previously administered Algeria were pushed aside by the generals who took over.

This was the sensational development of the early 1990s that the Western media made out to be something completely new in the Middle East: the politicization of religious forces seeking to take power through elections. From this derives the West's conception of the Islamic Fundamentalist movement.

Was the Takeover Attempt a Plot?

To answer that question we want to relook at what went on in the early stages of the rioting. For example, it is important to note that when the clergy became involved, it was at the *behest* of the government; they did not *insert* themselves into the violence, seeking to stir it up. The government called on the clergy to calm the passions of the crowd, and initially that is what they did.

To be sure, *some* clerics did seem to take advantage of the situation. Individuals who were not of the official clergy, and who may have been associated with the free mosques, appear to have been (in a manner of speaking) working the crowds. Films taken during the disturbances show these people entering into colloquies with individuals in the crowds, which created a kind of give-and-take exchange and had the effect of getting the crowds involved.[15]

All of this would indicate that there *were* religious figures who agitated against the government. That in itself, however, would not prove prior planning; that is, it would not be proof that personnel from the free mosques (if indeed they were from there) deliberately provoked the rioting as a means of seizing power. If one could show that these suspect imams and whomever it was they were interacting with in the crowds actually colluded, that might prove the riots were manipulated as part of a plot; however this has not been shown. Indeed, this long after the fact, it is still not certain who the individuals embedded in the crowds were. They have been made out to be *mujahadeen*.[16]

The mujahadeen were youths who went to Afghanistan to fight against the Russians. By 1992, many of them had returned home and thus would have been available to take part in the disturbances. The judgment, however, that the agitators were ex-Afghan fighters is based on impressions, such as the way they were dressed. The youth wore the traditional *gallabeya* and affected shaggy, unkempt beards. This was a style of the mujahadeen, but it was also an affectation that had spread widely throughout the Middle East about this time; in other words, the reversion to traditional dress predated the mujahadeen phenomenon.

Public displays of piety (manifested by a certain way of dressing) had been commonplace throughout the region since at least the early 1980s. The trend was in part fueled by religious sentiment, but it also seems to have had an economic basis.[17] For example, women in Egypt and elsewhere were going out to work, and in half-primitive environments were subject to constant harassment. To fend off unwanted advances, they affected religious garb.[18]

Thus, the theory (that the mujahadeen were at the heart of the disturbances), which certainly appeared promising when first put forward, remains unproven. And with no other obvious candidates who can be implicated, the plot theory cannot stand.

The Character of the Movement

The religiously connected individuals drafted by the crowd to take over the movement were Abbas Madani and Ali Bel Hadj; the one an intellectual, the other a fiery orator. These two steered the people into party politics. Largely on their own authority (it would appear), they induced the activist element in the crowd to pursue power *within* the system.

This has to be seen as significant. The movement did not *confront* the government. It did not seek to produce clashes, which it well could have done given the history of Algeria, a society that had experienced one of the few successful popular revolts of the post–World War II period.[19]

As to why it did not do any of these things, a possible explanation is the religious had been burned previously. The clergy had played a role in the original 1960s revolt. Afterward, secularists took charge and purged the clerical element. Some clerics went into opposition only to be ruthlessly eliminated. (The last surviving religious opponent of the regime to have remained active was killed in 1987 and, before his death, had been reduced to robbing banks to keep himself going.)[20]

In any event, the newly formed FIS chose to compete for power within the system, and this is what ultimately proved its undoing. When the army stepped in and abrogated the election process, the FIS not only accepted the result, it forebore to go back into the street. After that, the military—in a phrase—rolled it up. Bel Haj and Madani were jailed, as were a host of other individuals prominent in the movement.

Subsequently the religious opposition in Algeria languished. Its attempts to reassert itself were to no avail, and by 1995, the FIS had ceased to count for much of anything.

The FIS were replaced ultimately by gangs operating as guerrilla organizations. Although the gangs professed to be keeping up a form of resistance, it is doubtful they were in fact political; they seemed to comprise purely criminal elements.

The names of the gangs (the so-called Armed Islamic Groups [AIG], for example) are well known, as are their excesses. They have perpetrated terrible abuses, not just against the government but against their fellow Algerians as well. It is estimated that tens of thousands of Algerians have died in clashes between the gangs, the police and the communities fighting to free themselves of interference of the gangsters.

Egypt and the Muslim Brotherhood

In Egypt, the problem of dealing with religious opposition is not new. Egypt was where the original Fundamentalist society, the Muslim Brotherhood, started.[21] Egyptians will tell you that ideological agitation is exported thence: "Egypt doesn't *im*-port ideologies [they will tell you]; it *ex*-ports them."

Because of their familiarity with the phenomenon of religious activism, the Egyptian authorities have developed ways of handling it. Under President Gamal Abdel Nasser, this was done ruthlessly. Nasser smashed the Brotherhood after it allegedly had tried and failed to assassinate him. The pogrom initiated in the wake of that attempt was awful. Thousands of Brothers were driven into exile. Those were the lucky ones; the ones rounded up and jailed suffered bestial treatment.[22]

At the same time, many of those who escaped did very well overseas; many went to the Gulf, where they made fortunes in association with the local sheikhs.

Then, when President Anwar Sadat ejected the Russians from Egypt in the 1970s and instituted the *infitah* (essentially a turn toward free enterprise, away from dirigisme), he summoned the exiled Brothers to return. Sadat intended to make them a counterforce to the recalcitrant Nasserists in his government. In particular, Sadat wanted to check the power of pro-Soviet officers in his military.[23]

Many Brothers did return, and, as Sadat envisioned, they invested in Egypt's new free enterprise system. They also—as Sadat intended—got involved in politics, though not as he would have wished them to.[24] Instead of allying openly with him, they infiltrated the professional syndicates that flourished in Egypt under Sadat. They made the syndicates the foci of antigovernment activity, much as had been the case with the free mosques in Algeria.

Even with their own businesses, the Brothers played politics. They hired solely on the basis of religious conviction: only devout Muslims found employment with the Brothers.[25] Moreover, the Brothers established businesses mainly in Upper Egypt, a traditional area of Fundamentalist activity.

Ultimately, Sadat awoke to the danger posed by the Brothers; at which point he emulated his predecessor's action of crushing them. This may have cost him his life; many in Egypt believe that the Brotherhood paid for the bullet that killed the Egyptian leader.[26]

A badly shaken Hosni Mubarak, who succeeded Sadat, instituted his own harsh crackdown, but after a while he relaxed. The president agreed to legitimize a number of previously outlawed political parties. Mubarak held what he described as free elections, in which the Brotherhood was allowed to compete; however, the society had to run candidates on the Socialist Party ticket.

Mubarak's course of action resembles what went on in Algeria. Both governments opened the electoral process and allowed religious parties to participate. In Algeria, this led to a near takeover of the system by the religious. Why did the same not occur in Egypt?

One has to understand *how* the opening was managed in Egypt. It was not a true democracy that Mubarak instituted. It was what the Egyptians called *multipartisme*, a system democratic in form but with hardly any content. Whereas parties were allowed to operate, they were not permitted to organize at the ward level; essentially they were personality cliques and few had a program. Similarly, although parties were permitted to publish papers, they could not criticize Mubarak or even (under some circumstances) his government.

Whatever construction Mubarak may have put on it, Egypt was (and remains today) a police state. The security forces run the country under the stern rule of the *ra'ees* (that is, the boss), who is, of course, Mubarak. When Mubarak came to power the security establishment was already immense, and Mubarak merely added to it. Ordinarily, the security forces remain out of sight, only coming into play when trouble strikes. But then they are everywhere—in front of the major hotels, in all of the *maidans* (squares). One even finds them stationed along the autobahns at regular intervals.

And what are they looking for?

Popular unrest.

Among the Egyptian authorities there is fear of an Algeria-type explosion, a fear that is by no means groundless. Egypt is an extremely poor country. With a paucity of cultivatable land and a population of 70 million people, it is for many a constant struggle to survive. Egypt has some oil and natural gas, but this was only beginning to be exploited in the early 1990s and, even now, is not nearly as profitable as similar operations in the Gulf.

Consequently, Egyptians under a free enterprise system, such as Sadat tried to institute, are vulnerable. They were so even under Nasser, but with the difference that the Nasserists subsidized the poor. The Nasserists also, through their sequestration policy, milked the rich, which gave Egypt the appearance of being a classless society and that may have eliminated the recruiting grounds for violent protests.

In the late 1970s, when Sadat made his famous approach to Israel, the oil sheikhs of the Gulf cut off his subventions. This put his regime immediately into difficulty. Sadat appealed to the IMF for support, and the Fund agreed to help out, while at the same time ordering reforms. It wanted, for example, the virtual elimination of the old, Nasser-imposed subsidies.

Not wishing to rebuff the bankers but at the same time unwilling to go along (because he very much feared the result), Sadat complied in a heavy-handed way that provoked crisis. Sadat's intent, apparently, was to goad the public into reacting against the Fund's policies and then to exploit the unrest in order to avoid complying with the Fund's demands.

Unfortunately for Sadat, he underestimated the degree of popular resentment against him; he was unable to control the response he provoked. Mobs raged through downtown Cairo, trashing the symbols of the rich. Under the infitah, a class had developed that was ostentatiously wealthy.[27] The crowd seized on the things of this class and destroyed them.[28]

It is hard to imagine that Sadat could have retained many illusions as to how the people regarded him after this episode. Unfortunately for him, he did not have long to act on his newfound insight. By 1981, he was assassinated by a religious fanatic.

The New Class

Mubarak was able somewhat to relieve Egypt's economic plight by, in effect, signing on for service in the first Gulf War. This prompted a grateful

United States to reduce Egypt's debtload. Going into the war, Egypt carried $7.8 billion debt owed to the United States for aid under various programs. After the war, all of that was wiped off the books.

Eliminating this burden was a relief, but who can say whether Egypt was better off afterward? Mubarak, as head of Egypt, had a position to uphold as the leading Arab Nationalist. By setting the Iraqis up for defeat (and the Egyptians had, as we will see, a large hand in accomplishing this), the Arab Nationalist cause was irreparably harmed, and ultimately, Egypt's power position in the Middle East has suffered.

To be sure, Egyptian cooperation with the Americans did not begin with this; it started back with Sadat. Indeed, by this late date (1992), the Americans had infiltrated practically every level of Egyptian society. In particular, they had established ties to the officer corps.

Co-opting the military was done through the country-to-country missions. The Egyptian military trains with U.S. troops; it is armed with U.S. weapons; it shares intelligence with the United States. As a consequence, Egypt tends, in most instances, to follow Washington's lead, and it is hard not to believe that individual officers have been outright suborned.

In any event, the close association with the Americans nullified the military as an instrument of the popular will: it cannot fight the only enemy Egypt has, or at least that the people regard as such, because that one, Israel, is protected by the Americans. The Mubarak regime is hard-pressed to rationalize this paradox, which, as we will see, weighs heavily on Egyptians' consciousnesses.

In the meantime, the army, or at least the officer corps, lives well. Egypt's military establishment constitutes the bulk of the country's middle class, a fact manifested spatially. The officers live in model cities outside of Cairo. There, they have access to exclusive boutiques, grocery shops, mechanics' garages, and banks. The officers and their families need never go among the teeming masses of downtown Cairo. And here, one can argue, is the source of much of Egypt's present difficulty.

The Spark

As the author pointed out earlier, under Nasser, Egypt bore the aspect of a classless society. A feature of this was the fact of few areas of the capital being off-limits to the poor. Indeed, the heart of Cairo was poor man's turf, so to speak. The Nasserists built an elevated *ramblas* that encircled Tahrir Square, the hub of downtown. Here, in the evening (under mercury lamps casting an eerie, oliaginous glow), mobs of Cairenes strolled proprietarily through the city center.

This, to Sadat's way of thinking, was inappropriate, the affect being offensive to tourists. In the mid-1970s the ra'ees ordered the dismantling of the ramblas to open up the city space. Indeed, Sadat embarked on wholesale clearance operations all over downtown. These had the effect of driving the poor out of their neighborhoods, which in most cases they had inhabited for decades (if not centuries), and which were then bulldozed to make room for expensive high rises.

The result was to produce crowding in the outlying districts, where many former denizens of the downtown who were Sunnis, found themselves living cheek-by-jowl among Coptic Christians.[29] That apparently is what triggered the first alarming outbreak of religious strife referred to above. Knifings, the pillaging of Christian-owned jewelers, and even the torching of churches and mosques all occurred.

At this point no one believed that the violence was organized. That conviction set in later, the first signs of such trouble appearing in Middle and Upper Egypt.

Sadat's campaign to promote tourism included the amelioration of conditions in the major tourist areas, particularly the up-country region of Luxor. The Luxor area, which includes Asyut and Minya, was the same to which the Brothers had repaired to set up businesses with the aim of exploiting the conservative population.

Upper Egypt was the bastion of the blind sheikh Omar Abdur Rahman.[30] The sheikh, an inveterate foe of the government, had opposed Nasser and his successors. If ever it could be said organized religious opposition existed in Egypt (that is, opposition committed to bringing down the government by force), it was with this man and his followers.

Up-country Egyptians despise so-called *khawajas* (foreigners). They loathe foreign women in particular, who came among them half naked (in the Egyptians' eyes), acting in ways the men find provocative. As late as the 1980s, tourists who did not watch themselves in this area could end up being mobbed.

The Egyptian police, when ordered by Sadat to render the region "tourist friendly," went at it with a vengeance. Whole areas were purged, an activity that (as might have been expected) provoked fierce retaliatory attacks. Youths secreted themselves in seemingly impenetrable cane brakes, from which they ambushed policemen, picking them off with ancient fowling pieces.[31]

In response, the police unleashed an even greater assault, which ended by driving many of the wilder spirits to flee to Cairo where they went underground in the so-called baladi quarters. Effectively, neighborhoods like Imbaba and Bulaq became safe havens for outlaws on the run.

Imbaba and Bulaq are ghettos situated within the limits of the capital, but, in sociological terms, light years removed from it. The denizens are disaffected from the government—from which they neither get nor expect anything, and it is only under duress that the government can extract anything from them. In short, the neighborhoods were ideal places in which to hide.

What was wanted was an event that would force the impacted communities into confrontation with the government. This came in 1992, when Cairo was hit with a strong earthquake. The bureaucracy failed, signally, to administer aid, and rioting erupted. Subsequently, it was the religious who appeared to distribute food and blankets.[32]

Mubarak was embarrassed by the upstaging by the religious, and evidently, he was convinced that the Brotherhood, which organized the effort, sought to derive political capital from it. Indeed, the Brothers used the quake to bolster their demand to compete as labeled Brotherhood Party members at the polls.

The ra'ees cracked down. Mubarak ordered the police to shut off the Islamic charities, but then the populace resisted with more rioting, led by gallabeyaed youths, of the same type as were active in the Algeria disturbances.[33]

After this, violence between the police and the neighborhoods escalated. For example, the perpetrators deliberately penetrated tourist-frequented districts of the capital to commit outrages there. In 1993, a bomb exploded at a cafe adjacent to the Egyptian Museum, in the very heart of downtown, killing and injuring several tourists.[34]

The police attributed the attacks to the so-called Islamic Groups (*gam'iya al-Islam'iya*), which the police linked to the Brotherhood (and which Western journalists subsequently tied to the mujahadeen). That provided an excuse to purge the religious community, including the re-ligiously dominated syndicates.

There then ensued a vicious crackdown by the authorities on the Muslim centers of power, which included the ghettoes where the youths were based. At the same time it is noteworthy that, for all of the violence inflicted on it, the Brotherhood refused to be drawn into open opposi-tion. The organization's Supreme Guide insisted he would not confront the authorities; he wanted only to work within the system (he said). No matter how many charges were heaped on them, the Brothers professed themselves to be law-abiders.

Eventually an accommodation of sort was effected between the au-thorities and the Brotherhood, whereby the society was again allowed to function. At the same time, the Brothers were made to disassociate them-selves publicly from violent elements with which they supposedly were allied. The latter were rounded up in droves and put on trial. By 1995, the religious-based violence inside Egypt had to all purposes disappeared.

Israel, the PLO, and Hamas

The situation in the Occupied Territories is vastly different from that which obtained in the Magreb. In the latter area, the Arabs at least were ruled by their own kind. The problem was that all of the regimes across the Magreb were secular/military, and the officers had (in the eyes of the people) lapsed into corrupt ways.[35]

In the Occupied Territories, the Arab population chafed under alien (non-Arab) rule. To appreciate the extent of this discomfort, one has to understand something of the background of events.

The Occupied Territories originally were parceled out between Jordan (the West Bank and East Jerusalem) and Egypt (the Gaza Strip). When in the 1960s, Israel occupied these areas, Egypt for a while upheld, but then renounced, its claim to Gaza. Jordan did not renounce the West Bank and East Jerusalem until the 1980s, when at an Arab summit it was pressured to do so by the rest of the Arab states.

By shucking off Gaza, Egypt put the Palestinians, resident there at risk. They were now, in the eyes of the world, stateless individuals. Were Israel to drive them out, as was done in 1948 and 1967, they would perforce become wanderers on the face of the earth, so to speak. One has to bear this in mind, since it influences much of what later happened with these people.

There was no *intifadah* up to 1987. The Palestinians in the Territories lived more or less resignedly under the occupation. They were, after a fashion, taken care of in as much as they were employed. Thanks to the United Nations Relief Works Agency (UNRWA), the Palestinians were relatively well educated. Many had exceptional artisanal skills, and, because of their uncertain status, they were prevented from unionizing, hence the Israelis could look on them as a dependable resource of cheap labor.

Then, in 1982, Israel's Likud Party ordered an invasion of Lebanon with the intent of driving the Palestinian Liberation Organization (PLO)—which had bases there—not only out of the area but out of the entire Middle East. The Israelis somewhat succeeded in this. The Palestinian leadership ended up in Tunisia, a whole Mediterranean away from the people that it was pledged to serve.

Then, in the late 1980s, the Soviet Union started relaxing restrictions on the emigration of Jews, large numbers of whom either elected or were coerced into coming to Israel.[36] Once there, as many as possible of these were shunted to the territories to live in too-close association with the Palestinians. In the Israelis' eyes, the latter were expendable; on the slightest pretext they would seek to expel them, which, of course, also made room for more Jewish settlers.

All of this added to the stresses of the Palestinians. Their anxiety level increased when, also in the late 1980s, Ariel Sharon, then Housing Minister, launched an ambitious settlement (for the Palestinians, read "clearance") program.

Now the Palestinians were pressured in earnest. Instances of harassment between Israelis and Palestinians increased. Then an incident occurred in which an Israeli driver "struck" (Jewish version), "rammed his car into" (Palestinian version) a truck carrying Palestinian laborers, killing several.[37]

This provoked rioting by the Palestinians. The Israeli security forces, being unschooled in crowd-control methods, botched the suppression, and quickly the rioting spread. This was the start of the intifadah. Before the first intifadah was over (there was a second, we will discuss later) more than a 1,000 Palestinians died.

Significance of the Intifadah

The name, *intifadah*, is misleading. In Arabic, intifadah means frisson, spasm, or shudder. Given the awfulness of the thing, a much more apt designation would seem to have been *inkilab*, or *thawra*, meaning "uprising" and "revolution," respectively.

The intifadah designation was chosen by Yassar Arafat and the Palestinian leadership, who misjudged the character of the event. Because they originally underestimated its importance, they gave it a deliberately denigrating label.[38]

This shows the degree to which Arafat and his minions, tucked away in Tunisia, far from the uprising, had fallen out of touch. By the time the leadership realized that something more serious was afoot, they were almost too late to engage, which, as self-styled leaders of the movement, they would want to do.

The PLO attempted to infiltrate its own operatives into the territories, but this was not easy, as the Israelis were on guard against them. A potential leadership existed outside the green line (separating Israel from the Occupied Territories). However, it was handicapped trying to take charge: the PLO wanted a so-called "white intifadah," essentially a nonviolent revolt, and the community, stung to a fury by the harassment it had undergone, was bent on violence.[39]

It was then that the religious entered the picture. The Jordanian wing of the Muslim Brotherhood had been active in the territories for years. Indeed, the Israelis had encouraged the Brotherhood's presence there, reckoning that the society, as an avowed foe of secular Arabism (including, and perhaps, especially, the PLO), could prove useful.

Over the years, the Israelis cooperated with the King of Jordan (the principal supporter of the Brotherhood) to promote the cause of religious reaction, both on the West Bank and in Gaza. The Brotherhood effectively undermined the PLO by providing welfare services with a minimum of bureaucratic hassling and no corruption.[40] The Israelis, who were not much interested in helping out the Palestinians, were only too glad to have the religious take over in this department.

Then, when the intifadah erupted, the Brotherhood found it expedient to hive off, as it were, a wholly new organization, Hamas, which inserted itself into the battle. For a time, Hamas sought to calm the popular passions, much as had been done in Algeria. However, when, in October 1990, some Jewish Fundamentalists attempted to stage an incident at the Muslims' shrine of Al Aqsa, rioting erupted and twenty-one Palestinians were killed. At that point, Hamas (which was, after all, a religious group) turned on a dime, so to speak.

Peaceful demonstrating ceased as the Hamas activists exhorted the crowds to defend the sacred ground of Al Aqsa. It was from this juncture that the transformation of Hamas from a largely peaceful to an avowedly violent organization can be dated.[41]

For a time, Hamas maintained its close association with the Jordanians, which is to say, with the Jordanian branch of the Brothers. A perceptive commentary by an Israeli described the tie thusly:

> A so-called parlor leadership existed [he said], which resided inside the Green Line. Comprising well-known figures, this leadership spoke in the name of the *intifadah*, and—at the time—actually did control things. The parlor leaders, known for their long service to the cause, were respected, and as a consequence, could command obedience. Under them, a second echelon of leaders inside the territories operated underground. And below them, a third echelon of "street leaders," comprising thousands of youths, led the riots, performed acts of sabotage against the occupation authorities, and, in effect, were the foot soldiers of the *intifadah*.[42]

But as the Israelis put more and more pressure on the Palestinians, religious groups like Hamas and Jihad found their ties to the world outside the territories increasingly attenuated.

Then, under Yitzhak Rabin, the Israelis tried a new tactic of arresting Palestinian males wholesale, the idea being, evidently, to get them off the streets and into the jails. It mattered little whether those arrested were guilty of anything; on any pretext they were incarcerated. With all the adult males having been rounded up, the Israelis reckoned that the intifadah soon would wind down.[43]

Instead, the street fighting was taken up by the very youthful members of the community—mere kids, many of them not yet in their teens. Meanwhile, inside the Israeli jails, the incarcerated adult Palestinians fraternized, religious with secular; apparently a lot of proselytizing went on. We know the Jihad organization greatly expanded its membership because of this prison-bonding experience.

Thus, the structure of power inside the territories underwent an overhaul. As the ties of the community to the outside world languished, the new structure assumed a form adapted to the changed conditions. Most notably, a generational shift developed as younger fighters took command. In fact, the resistance inside the territories came to be dominated by street gangs.[44]

Meanwhile, in August 1993, Arafat and Rabin announced the signing of the Oslo Accords, after which Hamas and the other religious groups (principally Jihad)—in as much as they rejected compromise—found themselves isolated. The mood of the Palestinians after Oslo did not embrace violent resistance, not as long as there appeared to be a legitimate offer of settlement on the table. For a time, the religious inside the territories lay low.

However, they came back into action once the peace process collapsed. This was under Ehud Barak, with the Camp David debacle. We will have more to say about Barak and the supposed settlement that he, through the auspices of Bill Clinton, put on the table. For the time being, it is enough to note that the offer scandalized the mass of Palestinians, who erupted with fury at what they perceived as yet another sellout (both by their own leadership and the Israelis, not to mention the Americans).

But then in 1994, Hamas authorized a new tactic of suicide attacks on Israeli buses, and this marked a whole new phase of the struggle.

The Roots of the Problem

Having given an overview of activity in the three most affected regions, we now venture observations on the nature of the events described.

What we have seen in these three instances is a succession of disturbances, in each of which the religious figured prominently, but in not one could they have been said to have been the instigators.

The religious certainly threw themselves into the disruptive activity with a will; they sought to take charge of and direct it for their own purposes. *But they did not initiate it*, which calls into question the conventional wisdom-view of events whereby the religious supposedly plotted the upheaval for some years and did so in league with subversive forces in the Persian Gulf.

In the case of Egypt, the religious element surfaces only barely at first, when the Sunni Muslims turn on their neighbors, the Copts. But this confrontation practically was provoked by the government's relocation plan. Later, the Muslim Brotherhood figures when it distributes aid to earthquake victims. But that, as we said, was almost certainly an electioneering ploy to pressure the regime into putting the Brotherhood on the ballot.

In any event, neither of these actions can be said to have been calculated; both appear to have been reactions to circumstances of the moment.

The Israeli case is even less accommodating to the popular view of events. Here, the Israelis practically introduced the religious into the territories, intending to use them as a kind of Fifth Column. They only lost the clergy as allies when Jewish Fundamentalists staged an action at Al Aqsa Mosque, which agitated the latent fanaticism within the Hamas forces.

Even in the case of Algeria, we cannot say that the clerics were fomenters of unrest. They appeared on the scene early, but they were *called* to participate by the authorities. To be sure, the call was directed to the "official" clergy, and the free mosque imams tagged along, as it were. But even these unofficial ones were not—at least in the early stages of the trouble—looking to instigate a revolt.

How do we know this? The insistence of the religious leaders on working within the system tells us so. If violent takeovers were planned, the religious missed what would have been the propitious moment to strike.

Still, there is the matter of all the money that flowed from the Gulf to the local communities (some of which ended up funding the free mosque network); that was activity that predated the violence and so could be construed as being part of a larger conspiracy.

Zakat

Actually there is a quite simple explanation for this money flow. The *zakat* is an ancient institution in Islam, dating back to the time of the Prophet, who enjoined Muslims to tithe for the good of the community. Under the provisions of zakat, charitable groups regularly importune wealthy Gulf sheikhs for donations.

Perhaps once a year, agents representing the religious groups travel to the Gulf from all over the Muslim world, visit with the sheikhs, and make appeals for funds. This, as we say, is something that has been going on for centuries, and so there is no reason for the sheikhs to question the solicitations.

Moreover, in most cases the sheikhs being dunned do not care where the money is going. If it ends up funding organizations that the secular regimes (like that of Algeria) consider subversive, this would not be a concern. The sheikhs have no use for the secularists, who are viewed by them as practically atheists (or communists).[45]

In order to prove a conspiracy, we would have to have evidence showing that the sheikhs were directing the flow of funds to places like Algeria, *with the specific intent* of funding subversive activities. We cannot do that, and indeed, it almost certainly is the case that no such directed activity was going on.

Ironically, originally, money from the Gulf was seen by the secularist governments as a windfall. It went to fund soup kitchens, neighborhood clinics, and employment centers for casual laborers. These were all areas where the state ought to have been taking the lead. But, as we said previously, the dirigiste regimes were strapped for cash; they were not performing well in generating the kind of revenue the countries needed to manage their affairs effectively. So the secularist leaders looked the other way when cash flowed in from the Gulf. And not only the Arab secularists did this, but the Israelis as well. The Israelis, who had no wish to spend their limited funds on Arabs' welfare, were perfectly content to let the religious handle such matters.

Of course there was a danger here, which at least the Arab secularists should have seen, and that was that the people would assign their loyalty to the religious, not the state. This makes sense given that it was to the religious that they applied when in need.

At any rate, this matter of welfare relates to what is probably *the* main question about the unrest: Why is it that when the violence does develop it is almost exclusively religious protest that we see?

End of an Era

One has to be aware that two things happened when the Soviet Union collapsed. First, all of the secular regimes that had been clients of the Russians appeared overnight to become vulnerable (we already have discussed this).

But accompanying that was something else. Shortly after the collapse, the United States announced that it wanted more open societies in the Middle East. Both states that were already allied with Washington and those that wished to be so would do well (the Americans said) to hold free elections.

Algeria's decision to open its political process came partially as a result of this. Egypt's decision to allow the Brotherhood to compete in elections there was another such response.

This decision of the United States was seen as a great opportunity by oppositionists throughout the region. Of course, as we pointed out in our discussion of Algeria, not all antigovernment groups could take advantage of this opening. It takes time for parties to form and to win constituencies.

However, this was not the case with the religious elements. Because of the welfare programs they had set up, it was possible for them to gain adherents quickly. People had had time to observe them over the years and had come to trust them, and most of all, they were impressed that the religious (unlike the secularist regimes) were not corrupt. Consequently, there were very many strong reasons to back them at the polls.

When the secularists realized their error in allowing free elections to be held, they immediately sought to backpedal, as occurred in Algeria—simply cancel the elections. And that is what produced the upsurge of violence.

The violence, then, took on a religious character because of circumstances, such as the fact that across the region the only organized opposition that could seriously compete for power was the religious. When the secularists sought to prevent them from making a run, popular elements objected by going into the street to protest.

What about the presence in practically all of the situations of militant young radicals associated with the mujahadeen? Is that not something that ought to arouse suspicion?

The Mooj

As we said earlier, many of these young militants had ties to the Central Intelligence Agency (CIA)-organized and Saudi-funded mujahadeen movement.[46] After the Russians had invaded Afghanistan, the agency, thinking to embarrass them, began recruiting Afghan guerrillas to form a counterinsurgency aimed at expelling them from the country.

The mujahadeen group, as it was known, also had a complement of non-Afghans, many of them were young Saudis.

Why so?

In 1973, after the OPEC Revolution, the Saudi government had undertaken to increase the country's population; Saudi Arabia went from a land of never more than 3 million to upward of nine million.[47] The new generation had come of age by the 1990s, and it was posing a problem for the Saudi leadership. The king had attempted to educate the young people; however, most who enrolled at the newly built King Feisal University studied religion, with the intent of becoming religious scholars.

Riyadh found itself with a plethora of not very useful young men, who, because they lacked any worthwhile skills, were practically unemployable. So they lay around, as it were, unable to contribute in any meaningful way to their country's development. At the same time, however, one had to be careful how one treated these men as they were potentially fanatical.

Eventually someone hit on the idea of sending them to Afghanistan. The Saudis, who were bankrolling the CIA's mujahadeen effort, expanded the recruitment drive, signing up many of their own youth. These young Saudis filled the ranks of what subsequently became known as the Arab Afghans.

Had the Saudi leadership restricted the recruitment to just these young people, the mujahadeen movement might have been contained. However, a complication developed that induced the Saudis to expand recruitment more widely.

The Iran Factor

When the Russians invaded Afghanistan, it was not initially the CIA that responded by raising an anti-Russian force. It was the Iranians. As we intend to bring out later, there is a sizeable Shia element in Afghanistan, and it was to aid this minority that Iranian Revolutionary Guards crossed over into Afghanistan to raise an anti-Russian revolt.

The Saudis, the CIA, and the Pakistanis all had reason to deplore this development. The Pakistanis and the Saudis have long regarded the

Iranians as competition in this part of the world. The Pakistanis do so mainly for geo-political reasons; with the Saudis it is more a question of religious rivalry. As for the Americans, they of course had no love for the Iranians, thanks to Khomeini.

The Saudis adhere to a rigid form of Islam, Wahhabiism, which traditionally has been at enmity with the Iranian Shias. The Saudis have always considered Afghanistan, which is primarily Sunni, part of their appanage. Hence, to offset the movement of Revolutionary Guards into the country, Riyadh offered to finance the transportation and maintenance of Sunni Muslim volunteers from lands bordering Afghanistan, who would go there to join the revolt.

This had the effect of adding a whole new layer to the recruitment pool, and at the same time, it was this decision to open the ranks to Chechnyans, Pakistanis, Indian Muslims, and others that promoted the idea in the Middle East that this was a jihad.

At that, the recruitment spread even further. For now Algerians, and even Muslims from as far away as Indonesia, began signing up.[48] The recruits from specifically Arab lands became known as Arab Afghans. So now we have two categories of fighters—the mujahadeen, who were Muslims and could have been of any race, and the specifically Arab fighters, the so-called Arab Afghans.

Aftermath

Once the Russians admitted defeat, the mujahahadeen effort wound down. The CIA stopped being involved, and the Saudis paid for transporting the young people home.

But what happened when the young people got home?

Obviously they faced the same enervating lifestyles from which they had hoped to escape by signing on for jihad. At the same time, however, they were not the same young men who went to Afghanistan. They were now professional militants, so to speak.

And it was while these young men were lying around at loose ends, one could say, that the Americans began promoting their scheme to foster democratic elections. This energized the Brotherhood, the FIS, and other such groups into competing, and, of course, in the process of rounding up votes, the groups would naturally solicit the ex-mujahadeen fighters.

The move backfired, however, because generationally, the young people did not at all mesh with the older leadership. The Supreme Guide of the Brotherhood at the time was an octogenarian; he shared direction of the society with colleagues equally advanced in years. These elder statesmen had no intention of promoting a violent seizure of power—they did not have the temperament for it. They had also—through their earlier confrontations with the likes of Nasser and Syria's Hafez al-Assad—been warned off that sort of activity. Nasser's crackdown on them had been awful; Assad's was, if anything, worse.[49]

The youth were of an entirely different mind. When the secularists had recourse to violence, the youth struck back, violence for violence. This, the elderly religious figures could only deplore, and rather than allow themselves to be stampeded into actions they felt would be suicidal, they backed away. They disavowed the young people's response and refused to associate themselves with it. With that, the movement of traditional Islam, which had been on the verge (it seemed) of seizing power throughout the Middle East, stumbled badly.

We have now given an overview of what was occurring in the Middle East in regards to the religious forces in the 1990s. We have followed that with observations on events. Now we would like to impose our interpretation as to what was going on here. We propose to explain it by positing a conspiracy, however one that is at odds with the popular wisdom-view. In fact, we propose to stand the conventional wisdom-explanation on its head. It was not the sheikhs who were stirring things up, but rather the secular/military rulers, with perhaps the connivance of the Israelis.

The Plot

The secular/military regimes may have been unpopular but they were nonetheless secure. As pointed out in our discussion of Mubarak's Egypt, his was a police state. Tunisia, under Zine El Abidine Ben Ali, was one also (the president was a former chief of security). And as for Algeria, which was run by a junta, that was repressive on the face of it.

As long as the regimes could keep the allegiance of their security apparatuses they had no cause to worry. But now, with the United States demanding free elections, there was cause for concern. It is unlikely that even one of them could have survived an honest poll, as was indicated by the case of Algeria.

The problem for the secularists, then, was how to defy the Americans without being seen to do so. A clue as to how they went about this was supplied to the author by an Egyptian intelligence officer. We met him in Algiers in 1992. The officer had been sent to the Algerian capital to meet the generals who had just taken charge there.[50]

According to this individual, Mubarak and Ben Ali (and also the King of Morroco) had warned the Algerians not to hold elections, and when they went ahead—and things turned out badly for the regime—the Egyptians sent the officer to advise on how to retrieve the situation.

Assuming his evidence is reliable, this would indicate that plotting was going on. Further evidence to support this view was later obtained in Tunisia, from pro-democracy campaigners.

Tunisia has for long had a vigorous pro-democracy movement (secular, not religious), which the oppositionists hoped to advance with support of the Americans. According to opposition figures, Ben Ali impugned their activity by manufacturing a plot against his regime. He claimed that the plot was hatched by a religious group, Nahda. According to Ben Ali, Nahda was a Tunisian variant of the FIS.

To show the group's malign intent, Ben Ali displayed weapons he claimed were uncovered by the police and that supposedly were cached by the militants. Nahda, Ben Ali averred, was set to provoke a coup when the ever-alert Tunisian police intervened.

The Tunisian oppositionists scoffed at these claims. First of all, the weapons were ancient (some actually seemed to have been homemade). Moreover, the leader of Nahda was a virtual nonentity—an old man, he was living in exile in France and had been there for many years. No one took him seriously as a force in Tunisian politics.

The oppositionists reasoned that Ben Ali was using the threat of Islamic takeover (à la Algeria) to crack down on the secular pro-democracy forces, with the complementary aim of evading having to hold elections.

In Egypt, at this time, Mubarak did something that also raised suspicions. He granted an interview to Western journalists in which he discussed a recent raid conducted by the Egyptian police on a mosque in a heavily traditionalist area of Upper Egypt. Police killed some twenty-one worshipers in the raid.[51]

In Muslim lands, one does not invade a mosque and kill worshipers, and if one (for whatever reason) does do so, one certainly does not boast about it. What was Mubarak up to?[52]

Evidently he was preparing the ground for an address he was going to give in a week's time to the U.S. Congress. Mubarak had been invited by Clinton to travel to Washington and address the lawmakers.

In his talk, the Egyptian made a startling revelation. He repeated the charge that the world was confronting a threat from radical Islam, but then he went further, claiming that the instigator of the jihad (Mubarak's term) was the Islamic Republic of Iran.

A few days before, the Israeli Prime Minister Yitzhak Rabin had also appeared before the Congress, and he had taken the same position; that is, that the West was under attack from Iranian-inspired elements.[53] Interestingly, both leaders offered their aid to the United States to wage this, as they called it, war on terror.

In the next several days, as Rabin and Mubarak stayed on in the United States, they granted interviews in which they repeated their threat-warnings. American journalists were impressed, as there followed a rash of stories dealing with Iran's alleged sponsorship of Islamic terror.[54] Not just the newspapers took up the theme. It was all over the television, and even academics became involved, holding conferences on the theme.

The fact that the campaign gained such publicity was remarkable, the more so because the allegations about Iran were completely untenable.

Why?

Islam is split between two major sects, Sunnis and Shias. Iranians are Shias; most other Muslims are Sunnis. These two have an enmity that stretches back to the beginning of Islam. It is therefore not credible that Egyptians, Tunisians, and Algerians—all of whom are Sunnis—would follow the direction of Iranians, who are Shias. (It is like saying that Scotch Presbyterians would look to Rome for leadership in a religious fight.)

If the claims of Mubarak and Rabin were so untenable, why were they given great credence? Something had happened that predisposed Americans to take the charges seriously. Terrorists had weeks before (1993) assaulted the Twin Towers buildings in Manhattan (the first such major atrocity perpetrated against the United States). This was an extraordinary occurrence for which Americans were avid to find an explanation.

Mubarak and Rabin identified a culprit whom the Americans were already disposed not to like. By saying that Khomeinism was responsible, they appeared to have cleared up a great mystery. Their explanation, as we said, was untenable, but few appreciated that. And when so many journalists appeared to take it seriously, there was no reason for Americans not to believe.

Of course, this leaves the matter of the Twin Towers attack itself. Who did that, if not the Iranians?

It is beyond the scope of this study even to speculate about this. But there are aspects of the affair that are strange and which relate to the matter under discussion. For example, at the trial of the accused bombers, it was brought out that a blind sheikh led them to perpetrate the deed—this was none other than Abdur Rahman, the same sheikh we discussed in regard to antigovernment activity in Upper Egypt. We described the sheikh as an inveterate foe of the secularists Nasser, Sadat, and Mubarak. It seems he fled Egypt during Mubarak's time and settled in Hoboken, New Jersey, where the alleged terrorists met him through a local mosque.[55]

Mubarak knew of the sheikh's presence in the United States. Indeed, he had tried and failed to have him extradited. The Americans had refused his request, which was seen as peculiar at the time. But then it was brought out (also in the trial) that Abdur Rahman was working for the CIA, as a recruiter for the mujahadeen.[56]

There was an even stranger development. It appeared that an Egyptian, spying for Mubarak, had infiltrated the bombers' cell and was, according to court testimony, performing a mentor's role for the accused (all of whom were young and inexperienced). The agent, Emad Salim, supposedly suggested the type of bomb to use and even helped procure the explosive material. It very much appeared that he was trying to entrap the youths.[57]

Salim disappeared just before the bombing occurred. However this was not the end of it. Until just before he dropped from sight, Salim had been reporting to the FBI; so obviously, then, he was a double agent. He was keeping the FBI apprised of the progress of the plot but had neglected to tell it when the thing was set to come off.[58]

And there we intend to leave it. A fog of conspiracy hangs over this business that (we think) needs to be pondered. It probably cannot be penetrated, not on the basis of information we have now. In any event, it is not worth spending further time on. For now we want to take note of what came of all this.

Washington backed away from its campaign of promoting free elections. The thinking seems to have been that, were the elections to be held, and were the religious to score significant gains (as was likely), this might not be to America's advantage. It might end up swapping reliable (but undemocratic) allies like Mubarak for a lot of potential terrorists dedicated to working against U.S. interests.

Once the United States backed down, the religious revival (which as we said was already in disarray) expired. Mubarak, Ben Ali, the Algerian colonels, the Israelis—all cracked down on the religious, and in a matter of months (with the exception of the Israelis) had disposed of them. By 1995, there was little religious antigovernment activity in Arab lands.

The Epistemological Break

Once the Americans in effect disavowed their pro-democracy campaign, the secular/military rulers, plus the Israelis, had no need of keeping on demonizing Islam. Indeed, propaganda to that effect slackened off, not only in the United States but elsewhere generally.

But then, three years later, the world was rocked by a horrendous explosion of violence, again arising from within the Middle East. The most spectacular event was the second Twin Towers attack. But that was just part of it. That outrage was preceded by other assaults on two of America's embassies, one in Dar es Salam, the other Nairobi, and an attempt on an American warship, the U.S.S. Cole in Yemen.

There had to be an explanation for this new round of outrages, and the Americans were quick to supply one. Unfortunately it was as half-baked as had been all of their previous explanations.

The Americans convinced themselves—once more—that Iranians were behind the business. In fact, they had been developing this explanation since 1995. That year saw the occurrence of a couple of, as it turned out, significant events. The first involved a sabotage attack on Americans in

Riyadh, in which five were killed. The next year, Khobar Towers, an American barracks in Dharam, was blown up and seventeen Americans died.

The FBI was called in to investigate both these occurrences, and it was the agents' theory that the Iranians were behind the attacks. The Saudis never bought this idea. For one thing, they were just then in the middle of a rapprochement with Tehran, but over and above that, they knew who was doing it—it was native Saudis.[59]

The Appearance of al Qaeda

When the U.S. Army entered Saudi Arabia in 1990 to use that country as a staging ground for the attack on Iraq, its appearance touched off a fierce debate among the country's *ulama* (religious scholars). Saudi Arabia is the venue of the so-called Holy Places of Islam, sites associated with the birth and career of Muhammad and which for that reason are especially revered. It is *haram* (forbidden) for non-Muslims to enter the Kingdom, much less be in proximity to the sites. Nonetheless, the royal family, with much arm-twisting, prevailed on the scholars to sanction the entry of so many U.S. military personnel, a concession that was only given on the condition that the Americans depart once the war was over.

However, when the war ended the Americans did not depart. And, as a consequence, it was not long before violence against U.S. service personnel began to escalate. The attacks in Riyadh in 1995 and at the Khobar barracks the following year were the first warnings of native displeasure.

When the Saudi government importuned the Americans to be gone, the latter at first seemed to comply. However, they were only temporizing. Finally, when the Saudis were driven to repeat their demands, the Americans pulled out of Sultan Air Base (just south of Riyadh), but only to withdraw into the desert. Apparently the Americans felt they were complying: out of sight, out of mind.

There were now up to 20,000 Americans in the peninsula. This was an immense force. It could not be hidden away, no matter how far the Americans withdrew into the desert. The Saudis knew they were there, and, convinced that the Americans were not going to leave, they evidently decided to step up their attacks, going after the embassies and the U.S.S. *Cole*.

This is when al Qaeda, and its leader Osama bin Laden, appeared on the scene.

Bin Laden

After the twin attacks on the embassies, evidence was brought forward implicating the al Qaeda group, and investigations were commenced into the background of bin Laden.[60] The results were startling. It was developed that, as had been the case with Abdur Rahman, bin Laden was associated with the CIA-sponsored mujahadeen. Only bin Laden had not been a mere foot soldier in that effort, as had been Abdur Rahman. Bin Laden was an immensely wealthy Saudi/Yemeni who had been a principal director of the American-sponsored counterrevolt.

After the Soviets were driven to depart Afghanistan, he had returned to Saudi Arabia and was there when the Iraqi war loomed. Bin Laden had opposed calling on the United States for troops to oppose the feared invasion by the Iraqis; instead, he offered to defend the kingdom with his mujahadeen.[61] The royal family had refused. The Americans came in and when, after the war was over, they did not depart as they had promised, bin Laden was incensed.

We must assume that this is when he joined the effort to drive the Americans out, and that it was he who was behind the attacks on the embassies and the U.S.S. *Cole*, and ultimately on the Twin Towers.[62]

This explanation is based a great deal on conjecture, because the facts that are essential to grasp what went on have never been revealed. However, what we are claiming has the merit of making sense without involving the Iranians (which involvement, as we say, is ridiculous). Also, there is no linkage between the attacks and a suppositious world-girdling jihad movement. Under our interpretation, this can all be set down to a simple matter of grievance. The Saudis looked on the Americans' presence as an abomination; they wanted them out. The Americans refused to go. Certain Saudis attempted to drive them out by initiating a series of escalating attacks, which culminated in the horrendous kamikaze bombings of the Twin Towers and Pentagon.

In other words, we believe these are two *unconnected* sets of happenings. The first eruptions of religious violence (in the early 1990s) are in the nature of a socioeconomic upheaval in which Arabs across the whole

Middle East protested against governments they regarded as corrupt, and when the governments responded with violence, the protestors lashed back, which led to an area-wide explosion.

The second set of attacks, commencing with the 1995 sabotagings in Riyadh and ending with the second Twin Towers assault and 9/11, is a strictly Saudi-engendered affair, which arose out of the perception on the part of the natives that their holy of holies, the sites at Mecca and Medina, were being profaned.

Now, the question to be answered—and the one that will occupy us for the rest of the book—is why did the Americans choose to ignore the warnings that could not have been more explicit, that is, that they should get out of the kingdom; dismantle their base, and depart? We believe that, had they done this, the second Twin Towers attack would never have occurred.

The answer we are going to come up with is that they would not depart because they had vested interests in hanging on, and those interests involved trading arms with the monarchs and controlling Gulf oil, neither of which, obviously, had anything to do with religion.

CHAPTER 2

Arms in the Gulf

In the last chapter we saw how religiously inspired unrest swept the Middle East in the 1990s and ultimately invaded the sheikhdoms of the lower Gulf, a fact that surprised many. That area had been isolated from disturbances that affected the broader Middle East; its denizens seemed immune from the political and religious excesses rife throughout the rest of the region.

In this chapter we want to show that this calm was contrived; it was managed through a system of constraints. The constraints were put in place initially by the oil companies that opened the region to exploitation in the 1920s.

When the constraints came off (as they did with the repudiation of the oil company concessions in 1973) the peace of the region imploded, and the area sank into deep discord.

The single event that triggered the eruption was the OPEC Revolution, but the revolution was not a *sui generis* affair; it had to be led up to, and to get at what precipitated the great upheaval, we will investigate the rise of nationalism.

The two major states in the Gulf—Iran and Iraq—both were affected with nationalism, which became a force in the Gulf in the 1930s. We will see how these two handled the development that subsequently brought them into conflict with the oil companies.

We also look at the career of Mohammad Reza, the last shah of the Pahlavi dynasty. It was he who practically single-handedly opened the Gulf to the arms dealers. The shah bought copious amounts of weapons, and in the process, managed to so ingratiate himself with Washington that by the 1970s he had himself anointed by Richard Nixon as America's Policeman in the Gulf, an extraordinary rise in status for a man the Americans initially despised.

Over the years, successive administrations in the United States have made much of the fact that peace in the Persian Gulf was secured by American arms. Supposedly it was U.S. readiness to provide weapons to the Gulf states (with which to defend themselves) that kept the region stable. One can understand why the Americans would want to promote such a view, but it hardly squares with reality.

When the Gulf was truly stable—and it was more or less so until the 1960s—it was kept that way by the international oil system, that is, the fact of the area states having entered into concessionary arrangements with the major oil companies.[1] This process, in which the rulers participated because they thought it was in their interests to do so, had the unanticipated result (for the rulers) of constraining their freedom. The constraints that the oil companies put on them were real and sufficient to preclude the rulers from gaining that which they coveted—the development of an aggressive military capability.

Working in concert with the British, the oilmen were, for a time, able to manipulate the royalties from the sale of oil so as to check the rulers' arms-buying capability, which of course directly impinged on the ruler's militarization schemes. To understand how the oilmen were able to succeed in this, we need to know something about how the concessions operated.

Tapping the Concessions

When the British went into the Gulf right after World War I they faced a peculiar problem. They wanted the area's oil. However, oil is an unusual commodity, inasmuch as production must be regulated if the commodity is to be at all profitable. This has to do with oil's omnipresence and its tendency toward developing conditions of glut.

The British had reason to believe the whole of the old Ottoman Empire was floating on one vast pool of oil, which obviously complicated their situation. With the automotive age coming on, and oil companies becoming bigger and bigger money earners, the compulsion of many to get into the oil business was intense. That meant Britain could look forward to increased oil activity throughout the region, and thus it sought to limit exploration to companies with which it had direct dealings (which is to say, those that were British).

Britain initially had but one working oil concession, which it acquired before World War I. This was in Iran (not a mandated territory, but something close to it).[2] This was the so-called Anglo-Persian Oil Co. (APOC). The British government owned 56 percent of APOC stock, which made it a quasi-arm of the state.

After Britain assumed the mandate for Iraq, it opened that country up to exploration by a newly formed company, the Iraq Petroleum Co. (IPC), and the principal stakeholder here was the APOC. The latter operated in partnership with the Royal Dutch/Shell Company.[3] Technically, Royal Dutch was not British. However, due to changes brought about during World War I, its status was ambiguous in this regard.[4]

In any event, there is no question that Britain dominated oil activity in both Iran and Iraq through the APOC and IPC. Had Britain been able, it would have restricted the whole of the northern Gulf region to exploitation by just these two. Unfortunately for it, the Americans disputed the arrangements in Iraq.

Almost as soon as World War I ended, American companies began hovering on the margins of the old Ottoman Empire, scouting concessions. Britain at first warned them off, but this brought the American government into play.[5]

Washington was at this time promoting the policy of the Open Door, claiming that American business should be able to operate anywhere; no "door" should be shut against it. That applied very much to the Middle East, because, in the Americans' view, the British were only in the area because of their participation in World War I. The United States, too, had fought in that war; thus Americans had as much right as the British to be there.

Because Britain owed the United States so much money for debts incurred during the war, resistance to American demands was futile. Ultimately, two American companies, Jersey Standard and New York Standard, were let into the region, into Iraq, specifically, where they became partners in the IPC.[6]

This situation of the Americans wanting to get into the Middle East to prospect for oil needs explaining. The United States supposedly at the time was the font of all oil production; America was where oil originally was made commercially profitable, and some of the biggest oil companies in the world were based there. Indeed, the two companies we are dealing with here, Jersey and New York Standard, were *the* biggest, the flagship companies of the old Standard Oil Trust.

It was precisely because of what had happened to the Trust that the Americans were ranging the world, seeking to expand their operations outside the U.S. borders.

Americans Demand Entry

After World War I, several of the former Standard companies that had been forced earlier to disaffiliate (thanks to the Sherman Anti-Trust Act) found themselves in a bind: the companies had not enough producing fields. Jersey, for example, the former banker of the Trust, had plenty of cash but few actual working properties. New York Standard was in a similar fix. So these two companies, and some other similarly disadvantaged ex-Standards, embarked on a worldwide hunt for new oil.[7]

Jersey made significant finds in Venezuela, but elsewhere in South and Central America came up short, thanks to the British having gotten into these regions ahead of it.

Britain's behavior after World War I toward acquiring concessions was extraordinary. London went into the war (as we said) with not much more than one field in Iran, but within ten years after the war was over, it owned a slew of concessions worldwide.[8] British planners had had the forethought during the war to make up for their country's oil shortage.[9]

On the other hand, American companies, which, as we said, were the original oil producers, had not been as prudent. Not thinking they were would encounter competition, they had made no moves to seek oil far afield and, as a consequence, had allowed the British to steal a march on them.

After the war, when the Americans realized their mistake, the U.S. government got involved. Reportedly the State Department urged the companies "to go and get it," meaning prospect for oil overseas.[10] Whether this in fact is the way it went, or whether the companies acted without having to be prodded, is uncertain. Whatever the case, we see the Americans expanding overseas, and eventually they land in the Middle East. The aforementioned showdown between Britain and the

United States came over an attempt by Jersey to prospect in Palestine. In response to British stonewalling, the U.S. State Department fired off a sharp note to which Whitehall replied in kind. It was only after a spirited back-and-forth of missives that the British backed down.[11]

Jersey and New York were not let into Palestine (fortunate for them; there was no oil in Palestine). Instead, they went, as we said, into Iraq, becoming part of the IPC.

The entry of the two largest American companies into a joint partnership with what were then the two largest oil companies outside the United States (APOC and Royal Dutch) was a tightly held affair. The British government lay down strict conditions for operating in the area controlled by the mandates.[12] One was that the Americans were not to seek properties anywhere else in the former Ottoman Empire without having secured permission from their partners.

As things developed, this did not become an issue. Shortly after this, the Great Depression developed, and the idea of opening up new fields made no sense economically.

Indeed, just before the Great Depression, the British and American companies allied in the IPC gathered at Achnecarry, Scotland, where they concluded the famous "As Is" Agreement, the effect of which was to regulate oil production internationally.[13] They took this step in order to control prices, a move that was feasible because the companies owned 70 percent of the world's oil production. This step of agreeing to regulate output produced what later became known as the Great Cartel.

The Americans' behavior in entering into these agreements with the British is noteworthy. In doing so they effectively defied their government. America's policy was (as we said) that of the Open Door—ensuring freedom of access for American business everywhere. And it was with this in mind, that the U.S. State Department assisted the Standards to gain access to the Middle East.

Jersey and New York Standard simply ignored their government's intention. In partnership with the Europeans, they drew a red line around the old Ottoman Empire, within which oil prospecting and the acquiring of concessions was to be regulated, not just for themselves but for anyone.[14] As one of the participants in the original agreement noted, "Never was the Open Door more hermetically sealed than this."[15]

At any rate, this was the style of the oilmen operating in the Gulf until 1973, when the OPEC Revolution forced the implementation of an entirely different modus operandi. The companies deferred to the British, letting them handle diplomacy throughout the region; the Great Cartel looked out for the business side. And as for Washington, not only did it not have a say in Gulf affairs, it seems purposely (by the oilmen) to have been kept in the dark about what was going on there.

Colonialism, of a Sort

We want now to talk about the specific relations between the oil-producing states Iran and Iraq, the companies, and the British government. The states were constantly importuning the companies, and by extension the British government, to give them a better deal.

The producers, had they had the option, would have taken control of their own production. They could not do it because they did not have the expertise to run the fields, not in the beginning anyway, and later on—when they became sufficiently knowledgeable—they still were balked by special arrangements the oilmen had made.

The concessions were run on a carrot-and-stick basis. On the one hand, the ruler was motivated to cooperate because of the benefits he could derive from so doing. At the same time, were he to defy the companies, he could find himself in considerable difficulty.

The benefits were not hard to discover. The concessions were let for a specific time (usually five years), and over that period, the ruler could count on amassing sufficient funds so he could plan. Money could be allotted for various modernization projects; he could, for example, plan huge road-building projects.

The difficulty also was apparent. For example, in 1933, the APOC cut the royalty for Iran's ruler, Reza Shah, because, this being the second year of the Depression, the companies' revenues were down.[16] It was the manner in which it was done that infuriated Reza. There was no warning; the company arbitrarily cut what it paid by a third. When Reza, in a fury, ripped up the concession, the British embassy quickly intervened, giving him to understand that he either got back in line (i.e., accepted the cut) or the British would dispatch a flotilla to demonstrate off Abadan.[17]

Nothing could more perfectly illustrate the vulnerability of the rulers than this. It came down to one's approach toward property (an attitude that we will expand on later). Was the oil in the ground, which was indisputably the property of the natives, the basis of the country's wealth? Or was the infrastructure that extracted the oil what was primarily important (and of course the foreigners legitimately owned that)?

Actually, the rulers were even more constrained than they knew. As was brought out when Iran nationalized in 1953, the real—the formidable—control was exercised through the companies' marketing system whereby oil was distributed. This, the companies had rigged absolutely in their favor.

In effect, then, there were layers of control the natives had to penetrate, and the intriguing part, as we will see, is that the oilmen were able to keep concealed from the rulers just how circumscribed they actually were. For example, the rulers could not figure out how the oil business worked. When, as occurred with the Iranians, they asked for an equity stake in the company so they could sit on the board (from which vantage they could see how operations were conducted), this was denied them.[18]

The rulers could not even learn how prices were set. The companies were all integrated affairs, meaning they did business with themselves—there was no arms-length bargaining. Hence, setting prices was done arbitrarily.

This kind of contrived obscurantism on the companies' part was probably in the beginning not too oppressive, because the money the companies laid out in the form of royalties was adequate to the rulers' needs. But the rulers were embarked on a course of far-reaching consequences, and thus were bound over time to clash with the foreigners.

The Quest for Autonomy

Were the rulers to have curbed their ambitions, they would probably have escaped censure. In fact they wanted more; they sought to gain their autonomy, and for that they needed a strong military.

The oilmen were not pleased to see the rulers acquiring armies, since these, assuming they became proficient, could be used against them. As long as the rulers were comparatively defenseless, they would have to depend on the British for support.[19]

Moreover, with a military capability, the rulers could take their countries to war against neighboring states, something that would detract from the oil extraction process. At a certain point, therefore, the oil interests were prone to make trouble.

Confrontations came over the issue of royalties and how they would be spent. To the ruler, the royalties were natural surpluses, a kind of floating resource available for special projects—among which raising and equipping an army certainly was one. The oilmen, as we said, were willing to go along with this, but only up to a point. The steadiness of purpose of men like Reza (and later, as we shall see, his son, Mohammad Reza, and the Iraqi, Saddam Hussein) brought the issue to a confrontation. All these figures antagonized the system by becoming too involved (in the oilmen's eyes) with their militaries.

It was the combination, then, of the surplus and using it to field a national army that made for the difficulty. So, we might say that, in effect, nationalism was the political expression of the ruler's search for a surplus.

Reza was the first to run into this wall. Toward the end of his career he began cultivating ties with the Germans. The British looked at the developing relationship with suspicion. They foresaw that the Iranian would try to emulate his neighbor, the Turkish leader Mustafa Kemal Ataturk, who had built an effective fighting machine using German officers as mentors—and then used that army to drive the British from the country.

The British summarily forced Reza to abdicate, packing him off to "voluntary" exile in South Africa, for which the Iranian people never forgave them (more on that later).

In the case of Iraq, the British (as we said) held the mandate, which empowered them practically to control affairs in that country. They therefore were able to thwart Faisal, the Hashemite king, effectively. They would not allow him to acquire sufficient weapons to equip an army, which led Faisal to complain that he could not rule; his tribesmen had more arms than he did.[20]

For a while (between the two World Wars), the British and oilmen had their way on this issue; that is, on the matter of restraining the nationalist impulses of the rulers. And, ironically, there was a good result from it—there was practically no interstate conflict in the region the whole of this time. The oilmen would not brook any such disruption. Not until the OPEC Revolution, when the producers get control of things, does this situation turn around. Then we enter on the era of extreme instability in the Gulf.

Pressure on the System

The first significant attack on the concession system comes in 1950 when Iran nationalizes the APOC (which by that time had changed its name to the Anglo-Iranian Oil Co. [AIOC]). Since this episode becomes the touchstone of all future dealings by the Westerners with the Gulf States, we will spend some time looking into it.

In the period just after World War II, Jersey and New York Standard entered into arrangements outside the compass of the concession system that occasioned a series of events culminating in Iran's oil nationalization.[21]

Previously we said the system was grounded on the so-called Red Line Agreement, whereby the companies bound themselves to limit operations to three locales—Iran, Iraq, and Kuwait. Under the agreement, the companies would not venture farther afield, even though the whole southern sector of the Arabian peninsula below Kuwait technically was open to them.

Again as we said, these being Depression years, the companies had little incentive to increase production when additional supplies would have become a glut on the market. But just before the Depression, an American company—Standard of California—had gone into Bahrain and then Saudi Arabia and, in the latter, had found so much oil it could not market it by itself, and so it had had to call in a partner, the Texas Co.[22] Together they formed California-Arabian Standard Oil (CASOC).[23]

The story of how the California and Texas companies battled to get their oil to market over the opposition of the Cartel is long and complex. At one point they brought the U.S. government in on it, a maneuver that failed but not before Washington entertained the idea of buying CASOC, which would have put it in the oil business, the same as Britain.[24]

The affair of CASOC is significant as it gives further evidence of the power of business to coerce the U.S. government. When the American Cartel companies heard about the CASOC negotiations (carried on by California and Texaco with the U.S. government), they weighed in so strongly, Harold Ickes, who had been orchestrating the takeover, had to back down.[25]

After Jersey and New York Standard squelched the takeover, they sought to buy into the CASOC concession. Initially, their bid was opposed by the Californians, who wanted to go it alone. Undaunted, Jersey and New York appealed over the heads of the recalcitrants to the Rockefeller family, who (after the government-enforced breakup of the original Standard Oil Trust) retained large blocs of stock in all three companies.[26]

According to Blair, it was the Rockefellers who pressured the California interests into giving way, and the deal went through, with Jersey picking up 30 percent of the concession, and New York 10 percent.[27] The restructured company, with all four companies on board (California, Texas, New Jersey, and New York) became known as the Arab-American Oil Co. (ARAMCO), destined to become the world's richest corporation.

Complications Arise

The reaction to the American companies' coup from their fellow Cartel members initially was hostile. AIOC, in particular, was upset and of a mind to block the deal, which it could legally have done based on the Americans having agreed to the Red Line Agreement.[28]

Ultimately, however, the Americans made the British an offer they could not resist. The two Standards proposed buying large amounts of oil from Anglo-Iranian (Jersey 800,000 barrels of crude over thirty years, and New York 500,000 for the same period). AIOC, which lacked a marketing setup the equal of that of its fellow Cartel companies, accepted, and with that, the Red Line Agreement effectively was breached.[29]

The British were wrong to have become so exercised, as the first action of Jersey and New York after ARAMCO was formed was to insist the newly restructured company *raise* its price for oil to conform with that of the Cartel. In effect, this made Standard of California and the Texas Co. Cartel partners, something neither of them wanted but that was essential if control of the world oil industry was to be maintained.[30]

We are not interested in the intricacies of the Cartel relationship. Rather, we want to focus on how the deal affected the Iranians. In the long term, it led them to become alienated from the Cartel, and ultimately that led them to institute the oil nationalization. More immediately, however, the formation of ARAMCO seemed a good thing, since it brought more oil on to the market at a time when that precisely was what was required.

The Saudis Up the Ante

By the time the ARAMCO deal was finalized, World War II had just ended, and, with the introduction of the Marshall Plan, Europe was set to undergo a revolutionary transformation. A huge rebuilding campaign was about to commence that would be fueled by oil.[31]

Erstwhile arguments for conserving on production no longer were cogent. The Europeans could absorb any amount the companies cared to market.[32] Nonetheless, there remained the matter of whence the oil was to come. The Gulf was the most convenient locale, since it was close to Europe.

Thus the Gulf, which already had been favored by the Cartel (which had committed enormous sums to building up facilities there), now was to be even more favored—it would become the primary drawing area for oil to fuel the European recovery.[33]

It was at this point that the move of the Americans into Saudi Arabia began to complicate things. For the Saudis were rivals of the Iranians, who until now had had the lion's share of oil production in the region. The Iranians, as we shall see, were in no mood to brook competition.

Under the deal ARAMCO arranged with the Saudi ruler, Abdul-Aziz ibn Abdul-Rahman Al Saud (Ibn Saud), the company was bound to exploit Saudi fields on a rolling basis; that is, ARAMCO was supposed to surrender any fields to outside exploitation that it could not, or would not exploit itself.[34] With oil at a premium, thanks to the initiation of the Marshall Plan, and Gulf oil (for the reasons just cited) being particularly sought after, any number of companies wanted to come into the area. The king, who was receiving offers from several non-Cartel companies, was shrewd enough to exploit the situation.[35]

King Saud tried to pressure ARAMCO into surrendering undeveloped concession blocks. However, ARAMCO was not about to let outsiders into what it regarded as an exclusive preserve. Then, however, the U.S. government got involved, with the State Department counseling ARAMCO to make the concessions for which the king was asking. Surprisingly (for this was entirely out of character for the oilmen), ARAMCO agreed.[36]

This immediately came to be seen as a mistake—for ARAMCO. One of the new entrants, J. Paul Getty, in an effort to gain influence with the Saudis, made spectacularly attractive offers, which led the king to conclude that ARAMCO was not doing nearly as well by him as it should. So, he insisted that the company up the royalty.[37] Rather than pay the increase out of its own pocket, ARAMCO went back to the State Department with an ingenious, and somewhat devious, proposal. It wanted the U.S. Treasury to forgo taxes on ARAMCO's Saudi operations, because (the company claimed) it was already paying taxes to the Saudi government. Actually this was not true. The company was *negotiating* to get the Saudis to tax them, but it had not been agreed to yet. The money that the Treasury would forgive, in the form of U.S. taxes, ARAMCO would pay to Riyadh. That way the Saudis would get their royalty increase, and it would not cost ARAMCO a penny. The Treasury went along with this.[38]

King Saud ended up gaining what amounted to a 50–50 split, something that Venezuela had already gotten, but that the Cartel had resisted introducing to the Gulf. Of course once the Saudis got it, the Iranians were bound to have it too.

Anger in Tehran

Britain, the sole manager of the Anglo-Iranian Oil Company, could not afford to forgo taxes as had the Americans. Indeed, the American companies had only gotten away with it because the United States, at the end of World War II, was, in a manner of speaking, flush; it certainly was so compared to the British. Britain had fought two damaging world wars. It emerged from the first in a devastated condition, and had essayed to put itself back on its feet, but had not nearly succeeded when it was plunged back into a new, even more costly conflict.

Britain reckoned that taxes from Anglo-Iranian were one of the biggest sources of income it had. Indeed, it was brought out later that, under the royalty payment schedule Anglo-Iranian had worked out, the company actually was paying more in taxes to the British government than royalties to Iran.[39]

So, when the ARAMCO arrangement was revealed, the British saw trouble ahead. No love was lost between them and the Iranians. In Iranian eyes, the British had subjected them to numerous indignities, most notably the forced abdication of Reza and subsequent occupation of their country during World War II (even though technically Iran was a neutral in that war).[40]

A politically aware people, conscious of their illustrious past and of the fact that they now no longer could claim such glories, the Iranians were, in a word, prickly. Additionally, they were disillusioned with their leaders, the Pahlavis, who had, in the people's eyes, failed to safeguard the country's integrity.

Now the oil industry, the country's mainstay, had failed them too (or so it seemed). It rankled that the Saudis had gotten the 50–50 deal because, for all of the reasons cited in chapter 1, the Iranians regarded the Saudis as old rivals. Even before the announcement of the Saudi deal, the Iranians had been angling to increase their take, and this news of the Saudis' success only escalated demands for, as they construed it, justice.[41]

The fight was joined on August 1948, when AIOC sent a delegation to Tehran to begin negotiations. They stretched over a number of years, and eventually culminated in the Iranians' nationalizing the Anglo-Iranian Oil Company, which they did in March 1951.

At the time, this was something unheard of for a Third World nation. Indeed, this came to be viewed as one of the great national struggles of the post–World War II period, and the man who spearheaded the fight was an Old World statesman, Mohammad Mosadeq, who eventually became Iran's prime minister.

Mosadeq must be regarded as among the great figures in the Middle East after World War II. No question his influence was far-reaching. For all of his will and determination, however, the man was doomed; he was too far ahead of his time. Mosadeq believed that a country like Iran could go it alone in the world. He believed in self-determination, not just politically but economically as well.[42]

We will see, over the course of this study, that Mosadeq's philosophy made sense. The only effective way for a country to achieve autonomy is to take control of its natural resources. However, in the 1950s, this was a view that could not be upheld. Mosadeq ended his career a failure, but well beloved by the Iranian people.

Mosadeq and the young shah, Mohamad Reza, were not at all compatible. The antagonism may have derived from their differing backgrounds. Mosadeq was of the old land-owning class; the shah's father had been a sergeant in the Cossack Brigade, raised by the Czarist Russians. In any event, for most of their careers the two worked at cross purposes, which was unfortunate since both—each in his own way—were nationalists.[43]

Immediately Mosadeq nationalized the fields and offered restitution for the expropriated facilities. This, the oilmen refused. The companies took Iran to the International Court at The Hague, even though the court had warned in advance that it did not have jurisdiction in such an affair.

In the meantime, even though Iran kept the fields operating (which the oilmen had believed it could not do), it could not sell any of the oil it produced. Britain, acting on its claim that the oil was contraband, seized the cargoes on the high seas.[44]

America Butts In

One of the lessons of this study is how things fall apart if left unattended; one has either to pursue a firm policy or let matters lie. The Americans, in regard to the Iranian oil nationalization, dithered. Their behavior was a classic of confused diplomacy. They complicated matters, both for the Iranians and the British.

Early in the fight, the Americans took Iran's side. They did this in line with a longstanding policy of opposing empire; particularly they disliked the concept of imperial privilege, because that shut American business out of potentially lucrative markets (in a phrase, it was anti–the Open Door).

The Americans showed their support for Iran by appointing an ambassador to Tehran, Henry Grady, a staunch anti-imperialist.[45] His former posting was Delhi, and while there, he had backed the fight of the Indians against Great Britain. All of this the Iranians apparently took note of, and indeed, for a time it appeared that they might actually be following a strategy mapped out by Grady to foil the British.

Then the Americans did an about-face, which came in response to a change in the international political scene. In 1950 (practically coincidentally with the outbreak of the nationalization crisis), North Korea invaded South Korea; thus the Americans were saddled with a dilemma. They found themselves short of oil. Under the Marshall Plan, they were expected to supply Europe's energy needs; at the same time they had to supply their troops in Korea. Moreover, if the European recovery were to succeed, oil prices had to be kept down.

Faced with these demands, Harry Truman and Dean Acheson (his secretary of state) decided to call on the big oil companies for assistance.[46] They wanted the oilmen to take over provisioning the Europeans and the American forces in Asia. The companies would handle the logistics, while seeing to it that prices did not get out of line.

The oilmen agreed to this—*with a proviso*. They wanted the United States to withdraw support for Mosadeq; the Iranian was a "concession jumper," they said.

That was all it took for Truman and Acheson to reverse course. By the time Eisenhower took office, the United States was already distancing itself from the Iranians. Eisenhower severed whatever links could be said to have remained as he entered into a conspiracy with MI-6, the British intelligence agency, to overthrow the Iranian government.

The Communist "Threat"

The Americans never acknowledged that they had engineered a coup; they maintained that the overthrow was brought about by "popular forces" to thwart a communist takeover.[47] This was nonsense.

There was no effective communist interference in the nationalization crisis. Indeed, the Tudeh Party (the communist proxy in Iran) was a veritable awkward squad. It did nothing the whole time the crisis was on. To be sure, in the Soviet Union, Stalin had died, and signals were confused coming out of Moscow, so the Tudeh may have been prevented from acting due to circumstances.[48]

In any event, the public protestations of the Eisenhower administration that the overthrow of Mosadeq was a blow against communism had the effect, for the Iranians, of rubbing salt in the wound. They never forgave the United States, and indeed, the affair has become a lingering source of hostility, as alive today as immediately after the overthrow.

Cold War Effects

We stress Eisenhower's espousal of anti-communism because, as we shall see, this plays a part in practically everything that ensues. Indeed, Mohammad Reza makes the fight against communism into practically the leitmotiv of his dealings with the Americans. In this he can be said to have behaved most shrewdly.

We view Mohammad Reza as a kind of bridge-figure, someone who spans the two periods of Western influence in the Gulf—the initial time of British involvement followed by the entry of the Americans.

During the nationalization fight, Mohammad Reza had split with Mosadeq over tactics.[49] Just before the coup, the shah had actually left the country, in effect disassociating himself from the nationalization struggle.

When Mosadeq fell, the shah returned, expecting to be rewarded by the Americans, because, as he felt, he had picked the winning side. But when he appealed to Eisenhower for assistance in the form of substantial military aid, Eisenhower rebuffed him.[50]

This, the young shah found dismaying. After all, Eisenhower had couched his decision to support the coup in terms of Iran being threatened by communist takeover. Yet, here the Americans were withholding aid that, under the circumstances, appeared (to the shah, at least) to be essential.

To be sure, Eisenhower was a committed anti-communist, but he also was a fiscal conservative. After World War II, America encountered difficulty with its economy. Eisenhower was ill-disposed to spread America's wealth; he wanted first to balance the budget.[51]

One could say that Eisenhower exhibited in microcosm the essential ambivalence of Americans generally. They tended to take a high-toned stand on things, declaiming in an idealistic fashion, but with all their gaze was focused on the bottom line; which is to say, before all else, they were businessmen.

Americans' involvement with the Marshall Plan can be understood in this light. They wanted to rebuild Europe, but they also wanted to open it up (the Open Door, again) to penetration; they wanted to trade with the Europeans. Obviously that could not be done until the latter were on their feet economically.

At the same time, isolationist sentiment in the United States opposed getting too involved overseas, particularly with the Europeans. So Truman shifted the focus of the Marshall Plan to fighting communism, which opened up new avenues of approach for the Americans. In the minds of conservative Americans, communists were everywhere, and most notably, the labor unions in the United States were packed with them.

A crusade against communists (even though directed against overseas communists) could be manipulated to undermine labor at home. Indeed, once George Meany, the head of the American Federation of Labor, joined the anti-communist crusade, the labor unions were, in effect, gutted. Meany purged communists from the unions, an act that some would say stripped them of their most zealous adherents.

In any event, the shah seems to have twigged to this dissembling character of the Americans; his subsequent career in dealing with them certainly gave evidence that he had. The thing to do was to indulge their posturing, while getting in with them *businesswise*. This was the shah's focus from here on; it is remarkable the leverage he got from it.

Moving on Two Fronts

Specifically, the shah did something that was remarkable for Third World leaders of the time: he did not abandon going after aid, but he supplemented that activity with buying arms, and where he got the money for this is, for our purposes, the interesting aspect of the affair.

After the nationalization fight had ended and Mosadeq was overthrown, the Americans insisted on reorganizing the AIOC concession, claiming that, because of ill-will engendered among Iranians, the British should not be permitted to reappropriate the concession entire.[52] It made better sense, the Americans claimed, if the concession was restructured, with other companies being brought in. This way the Iranians would not have to confront a return to the status quo ante, a humiliation for them, something difficult—after such a hard-fought struggle—to swallow.

It is interesting that the Americans were so sensitive to the Iranians' feelings after toppling their government in a coup. But here, once again, we are dealing with their dual nature. Washington got Britain off the hook by paying off the Iranians to settle the nationalization dispute; for that it expected to be reimbursed. The American oilmen wanted in on the AIOC concession (previously a purely British setup), and they got it. Now they were not only set up in Iraq and Saudi Arabia but in Iran as well.

The British agreed to overhaul the AIOC concession. AIOC retained 40 percent, Exxon and Socony-Vacuum (the new names for Jersey and New York Standard) along with Chevron (the new name for California), Texaco, and the Gulf Oil Co., each got 8 percent; Royal Dutch got

14 percent, and the French company, CPF, 6 percent. This was later to be styled the Consortium.

These changes shifted the balance of influence in the Gulf; in effect, they boosted the Americans' stake appreciably. However, nothing was done to change the status of the Cartel. Since all of the companies (the French included) were members of the Cartel, they all, working in concert, could see to it that oil production and prices were controlled as they saw fit.

There was, however, one subtle, but important, change that came into play, which was to have a monumental effect down the line. It was a change the shah was able to exploit for his own interests. Mosadeq had set up an independent entity, the Iranian National Oil Co. (INOC), to handle the nationalization. That company was preserved under the new Consortium. A percentage of Iran's oil production was allotted to it, to dispose of as the shah wished. He took that mite and sold it on the spot market. This was an institution that had grown up outside the control of the Cartel, where companies outside the Cartel could dispose of excess oil, usually at discount prices. With the money from these sales, the shah bought arms—not a great many, because he was not making that much in the beginning. But as time passed and conditions changed, the privilege of selling on the spot market ballooned into something big and with enormous implications for the fate of the whole Gulf region.

The shah did something else that was shrewd, showing that he had learned from his encounters with the Americans. In negotiating arms purchases, he was careful to stress that the weapons would be used to repel Soviet aggression. In a manner of speaking, the shah was pandering to the Americans' anti-communist bias; this was, recall, the period of McCarthyism in the United States.

The shah could be said to have been exploiting two developing trends in the United States, because in addition to making himself out as a foremost anti-communist, he also was buying weapons at a time when the military/industrial complex was just getting started.

The Complex

Today practically all Americans are aware of the military/industrial complex. But originally (in the 1950s), Eisenhower felt it necessary to warn his fellow Americans against the institution, about which, it was presumed, they knew nothing.[53]

The complex grew out of a wartime situation. America went into the war against the Axis caught in the grip of the Great Depression. Part of its trouble was that the economy needed rationalizing, a move the Americans resisted. To them, competition in business was all, witness the Sherman Anti-Trust Act. However, over time, the economy had matured. Rather than needing more firms, it needed less, and it was because such rationalization was resisted that the economy was stagnating.

To be sure, oligopolies, like the Great Cartel companies, existed, and these because of their size were able to achieve marvelous economies of scale. Thus tension existed, between the larger, more efficient oligopolies and the numerous inefficient—but politically influential—small businesses (or relatively small, at any rate).

Then came World War II, and America, to defeat the Axis, encouraged the oligopolies to produce materiel for war. What America did was institute a form of state capitalism, à la the Germans under Hitler.

This new mega-form of business ultimately swept all before it. The conglomerate was set to become the new lodestar by which Americans would guide their economy. The quintessential expression of the type was the military/industrial complex.

Getting Started

The complex grew out of the aircraft industry back in World War I. The introduction of an air arm to America's military launched the concept of flight as both a strategic and a commercial proposition.

Originally, only a handful of planes were produced, coming out of workshops of outfits like the Wright Brothers and Glenn Curtis. These were handcrafted (literally), turned out one at a time, and delivered to the military—the overall industry patron. The Army Signal Corps was the first department to contract with the Wright Brothers (in 1908).[54] By 1918, $350 million had been spent to make 14,000 planes, and it had taken 175,000 people to make them.[55]

Then, immediately after the war, the aircraft business imploded. In 1922, the market for aircraft had dropped to 263, down from the 14,000 units we just cited.[56] However, the government was quick to intervene to, in a manner of speaking, save the airmen's bacon. The Air Mail Act of 1925 opened a fresh new source of public orders. It was not long before civil air production began exceeding that of the military. Whereas in 1925 there had been only 342 planes produced for civilian use (compared to 447 planes for the military), that turned around the following year—654 to 532, respectively.[57]

What was being established here was a pattern of America's air industry being government subsidized, a condition from which it was never able to escape. For example, Pratt & Whitney, a major engine maker, made 36 percent of its profit on navy contracts from 1927 to 1933.[58]

Now we come to World War II, where the industry really takes off. At the outset of the war, President Franklin D. Roosevelt set a target of building 50,000 planes a year. This precipitated a huge investment in plant and equipment, with a concomitant leap in employment; there was $16 billion in wartime sales and a peak employment of 1 million.[59]

As might have been expected, at the end of the war everything turned down again. By 1947, sales had plummeted to $1 billion, and employment had hit a low of 237,000.[60]

Ah, but then came the Cold War, with the fortuitous (for the industry) demand for missiles, which, finally and forever (it seemed) saved the day. With the introduction of missile technology the aircraft industry literally reinvented itself, changing its name to aerospace to reflect the development of the intercontinental ballistic missile (ICBM) and later the more deadly MX-missile.[61]

With the introduction of missile technology, the industry branched out in a number of directions at once. It moved into the field of communications through aerial surveillance, a direct spin-off of aircraft production, as was another whole new industry—electronics.

America's leaders frequently cite this propensity of aerospace to spawn new growth as justification for putting large amounts of cash into the business, in effect subsidizing it. The claim is made that aerospace produces jobs. It does and it does not. By spinning off related industries, it does. But aerospace itself is *capital* not *labor* intensive, because the industry turned its back on the techniques of pre-war Detroit and the Ford Motor Company.[62] Aerospace leans toward robotics. Moreover, the business has come to be dominated by academe; that is to say, scientists (white-collar workers) predominate over blue-collar types of Detroit auto production days.

All of this has relevance for the matter just discussed—the determination of business in the United States to outmaneuver labor. By promoting an industry where unions are small and largely ineffectual, the conservatives sought to ensure that working-class solidarity would be kept limited.

This is just a side issue, however. For the Americans, the main consideration was the profit potential, and here the possibilities were seemingly unlimited. According to Markusen and Yudkin, by 1965, the aerospace business was logging $15.8 billion in sales (half of that in missiles and space vehicles).[63]

Aerospace had become *the* growth industry of the United States. So great was the involvement of government with aerospace, Markusen and Yudkin describe the relationship as a "closet industrial policy." Not only was Washington guaranteeing the companies' profits, it would bail them out whenever they got into trouble (which, as we shall see, did happen from time to time).

All of this was transpiring throughout the late 1940s and 1950s, and it was during this period that the shah was positioning himself to take advantage of what was going on. Shrewd operator that he was, he got in on the ground floor of what, from his perspective, must have seemed a good thing.

The Communist Menace

The shah was a master of manipulating perceptions; he seems to have had a knack for it. What he could not do on his own, he had the good sense to hire professional talent to do for him. Conservative publications such as *Time* magazine early noted the shah's arms-buying activities and began to comment on it, favorably. Seeing this, the shah hired public relations firms in the United States to publicize his activities more systematically.

What the shah did was raise the specter of the communist menace right next door to Iran—in Iraq. There, army officers had overthrown the client of the British, the Hashemite dynasty. These self-proclaimed

republicans drew the shah's enmity. It is likely that much of the antag-
onism was geo-politically based, but the shah was shrewd enough to make
it out to be an ideological contest between himself (on the side of the
Free World) and Abdul Karim Qasim, the Iraqi ruler, being backed by
Godless communism. The shah played up the idea of Iraq being a Trojan
Horse, whereby communism was being smuggled into the Gulf.

The shah's claims were vastly overstated. Still, there was an element
of truth in what he was saying. Qasim did recognize the Iraqi Communist
Party and allowed it to compete in elections immediately after he took
power. He also bought arms from the Russians. But this was in line with
the then widely prevalent spirit of nonalignment, which we discuss later.
Once the general established himself, he curbed the communists; in fact
he made them his bitter enemies.[64]

Qasim proved himself a maverick in yet another area. In 1960, he
presided over the formation of OPEC. He summoned the heads of state
of Saudi Arabia, Venezuela, Kuwait, and Iran to Baghdad, where on September 14, 1960, after a week of intense deliberation, the leaders agreed
to cooperate against the Cartel.[65]

Monroe Rathbone, head of Exxon, had that same year arbitrarily cut
the royalties on concessions, thereby forcing an across-the-board cut by
fellow Cartel members. The oil-producing states, led by Iraq, reacted
angrily, and the upshot was that OPEC was formed to be a kind of
counter-cartel.[66]

But most radical of all, Qasim initiated the process of nationalizing
the Iraq Petroleum Company (IPC). In December 1961, he sequestered
95 percent of the acreage the oil companies had acquired but never
exploited, the concessions for which he proposed to auction to the
highest bidder. He did this because, in his words, the IPC had shut the
fields in.[67]

Just at the time Qasim took this step, a rebellion of Kurds broke out in
the north of Iraq, which Qasim blamed on the oil companies, a judgment
with which the author tends to agree. Moreover it is likely the companies worked in concert with the shah over this.

The shah supported the fight of a Kurdish tribal leader Mulla Mustafa
Barzani against the Arab leadership in Baghdad. Barzani initially re-
belled to acquire land at the expense of rival Kurdish tribes.[68] The shah,
however, in propagandizing the revolt, made this out to be a great nationalist struggle of all of Iraq's two million Kurds.

In any event, the timing of the revolt leads one to suspect collusion between the oil interests, the shah, and the Kurds. The revolt threw Qasim off balance, forcing him to dedicate already limited resources to suppressing the Barzanis and, by taking the army out of Baghdad to fight in the north, enabled disaffected officers to plot against him.[69]

The shah contributed to Barzani's fight by opening his border to the rebels; he allowed them to smuggle arms into the north. It was largely due to his support that the revolt kept going as long as it did, from 1961 to the present day.

As for Qasim, he died in a hail of bullets, shot down in a successful coup mounted by a little-known, barely fledged party (interestingly this was the Ba'th, which was to cut such a figure later on). Frankly, it is hard not to suspect that Qasim was the victim of "oil diplomacy."[70]

The Shah Forges Ahead

During the time Qasim was in conflict with the IPC over the nationalization, the Cartel shifted its production away from Iraq to Iran. This had the fortunate result, for the shah, of increasing his revenue.[71]

This capacity of the companies to shift operations worked for and against the producers. In this case it hurt Iraq but was immensely beneficial to Iran. At the same time, however, the shah's action of exploiting his neighbor's (Qasim's) distress reveals the weakness of the newly formed OPEC. Had OPEC been a true cartel, the rulers would not have allowed the oilmen to play one of them against the other.

In any event, the shah was quick to exploit the windfall by buying more weapons. He also consolidated relations with Israel, which was another shrewd move. The Israelis welcomed an alliance, as the shah could (and did) supply them with oil, for which they were starving.[72]

Thus we see, at this early date (the mid-1960s), the political complexion of the Middle East changing. The secular/military regimes among the Arabs were becoming equated in Americans' minds with communism. Opposing them, a coalition had begun to form of reactionary forces, which included Israel and the shah.

We want to say a word about this perception, because it bears on matters discussed in chapter 1, the pervasive enmity of the so-called traditionalists forces in the Middle East and the newer secular/military regimes.

The Arab Cold War

Starting in 1953, the world was exposed to the phenomenon of the Arab Cold War (a manifestation of a rift in Arab affairs) between old-line leaders and new claimants to power. The claimants were army officers who confronted the old leadership, which was, almost without exception, monarchist.

The battle was joined with the toppling of Farouk, king of Egypt, by Nasser and the so-called Free Officers in the early 1950s. Subsequently, the officers' revolt spread throughout the Middle East. An attempt also was made to overthrow King Hussein bin Talal of Jordan (which failed). A coup was then mounted against Iraq's King Faisal, Hussein's cousin, which succeeded, bringing to power General Qasim.

Although the shah was not an Arab, he felt himself threatened by this wave of ideological discontent. To the shah, the claim of the officers to be republicans was bogus. They were, in his eyes, communists. As we have said, this belief, although it could hardly be substantiated, spread to all of the Western capitals.[73]

One who helped promulgate the misperception was John Foster Dulles, Eisenhower's secretary of state, who compartmentalized the post–World War II world into adherents of democracy and communists. When Nasser (and then, one by one, the other Arab military leaders) embraced non-alignment, Dulles lumped them into the communist camp because, for him, there was no middle ground.

It also suited the British to hold this view (of the officers being communists) because everywhere the officers struck, a client of theirs went onto the dustheap of history.

By the time Qasim had overthrown the Hashemite monarchy in Iraq, a trend was established of sweeping away the traditionalist governments. This so alarmed Eisenhower and Dulles that, in response to the takeover in Iraq, they actually sent troops to Lebanon, supposedly to defend that country and Jordan should the "communists" move against either.[74]

Moreover, in sending the troops, Eisenhower had promulgated what came to be known as his doctrine: America would defend any pro-Western regime in the Middle East threatened "by communist takeover."

If the officers who were taking power were not communist, why did they excite fears of statesmen like Eisenhower, and produce an ukase such as the Eisenhower Doctrine?

To understand the threat—the real threat, not the manufactured one—one has to appreciate how the British ruled the Middle East. They promoted weak governments, generally monarchies, backed up by the religious leaders. This way, they ensured that, whereas the monarchs might retain the loyalty of the masses (who were influenced by the imams), the intellectuals, who, in British eyes, were the real troublemakers, would be kept down. In any event, weak monarchs would have to be turning to the British continually for assistance.

This was all right as long as the British could offer protection. But as Britain's economy deteriorated, it became less and less able to shield its clients. This inability was felt particularly once the sub-continent Indians got their independence in 1947, because Britain had used Indian troops to police the Middle East.

So there *was* a threat to the ex-clients of the British, but it had little to do with communism. Nevertheless, shrewd operators like the shah manipulated America's obsession with fighting "reds" to enlist its support against the Arab republicans.

It was in this way that Nasserism, Arab Nationalism, and republicanism all became subsumed in the minds of Americans as forms of communism. In fact, what the Arab Cold War was really about was the fight of the traditionalists—that is, the monarchs—against the military secular regimes.

This is an important distinction to understand; otherwise one tends to misconceive relations between the Arab governments. The surviving traditionalists are mistrustful of the secular Arab leaders. Abdullah of Saudi Arabia in his heart of hearts probably has not much love for Mubarak of Egypt, and the disrespect is returned (we saw some of this in chapter 1).

In any event, by muddying conceptions of what actually was going on, the shah (for he was one of the principal architects of this disinformation campaign) achieved an effect far beyond anything that he probably could have imagined.

The propaganda certainly appealed to the Americans, who were predisposed not to like the secular/militarists on other grounds. For example, the Americans could not but deplore the officers' dirigist tendencies. There was nothing there with which the business-minded Americans could sympathize. The willingness of government to intervene in the economy, to consider alternatives to the market—such ideas were anthema.

Along with this, of course, the Americans could not abide the officers' obtaining arms from Russia. But, as we said, this course of action was practically forced on them. The terms under which the Westerners were willing to sell arms were, to the Arab republicans, repugnant: Dulles wanted the officers to sign on to the anti-communist crusade, which they flatly would not do. A leader like Nasser was ideologically indisposed to exercise that option. In those days, nonalignment was popular among Third World leaders: Jawaharlal Nehru of India, Tito of Yugoslavia, and Nasser all stood for a middle way, neither East nor West.

In any event, the fact of the Arab officers getting arms from Russia alienated them from the military/industrial complex in the United States. So here on another front the officers were estranged, while the monarchies, by increasing American arms purchases, appeared as an attractive alternative form of rule.

It was in this way that the United States gradually, but surely, came over the years to support some of the world's most retrogressive and oppressive regimes in the region.

The Shah Maneuvers

The primitive Ba'thists who overthrew Qasim lasted exactly eleven months before they too were overthrown.[75] This time the claimant to power was an Arab Nationalist military officer, Abdel Salam Aref, and, although initially a partisan of Nasser, he eventually showed himself a sympathizer of the West. Unfortunately for the British and Americans, Aref died in a helicopter accident a relatively short while after taking power.[76]

Aref's successor, Abdur Rahman Aref, for a time tried to carry on the westward-leaning policies of his brother, but was forced to abandon this course after the 1967 Arab-Israeli War. After that debacle (for the West), Abdur Rahman reverted to radicalism, further nationalizing the IPC fields. This was the fight Qasim had started that he had been unable successfully to conclude.

A cabal of military men overthrew Aref. This lot of usurpers lasted only three days before they were betrayed internally, by Ba'thists again. Unlike the first Ba'thists, these were military men.[77] Although the Ba'thists were not disposed to embrace communism, they were more or less driven to it.

The Ba'thists were fiercely anti-Israel, and one of their acts on taking over was to stage a huge show trial in which, among the individuals accused of espionage, were a number of Jews. The international Jewish community reacted by staging a media campaign, tarring the Ba'thists as the 1960s equivalent of terrorists. This further estranged the Ba'thists from the West and moved them toward Moscow.

At this time, Saddam Hussein was a mere lieutenant of the Ba'thist ruler, General Ahmed Baker, but he was a young man on the way up. Baker appointed him to head the so-called Follow Up Committee to work out the terms of the oil nationalization, an assignment that conveyed enormous responsibility.

Saddam's contribution was to overcome what heretofore had been an apparently insuperable obstacle toward successful nationalization, namely, how to get around the companies' distribution system, which effectively prevented the producers from entering the market. The shah had resolved this problem partially by taking advantage of the spot market. But the shah was only in control of a small portion of Iran's overall production. The Iraqi Ba'thists meant to commandeer all of Iraq's oil wealth, and thus the disposal problem was a huge one, as long as the Cartel controlled the distribution.

Saddam utilized the tactic of barter. He worked out a slew of arrangements with Moscow, whereby, in return for providing technical assistance (for modernizing Iraq's fields), Russia got oil, which it then sold for hard currency to its Eastern European satellites.

This successful tactic naturally alienated the Ba'thists from the Cartel, but because of the timing of Saddam's move (he initiated it in 1972, one year before the OPEC Revolution) the Iraqis got away with it.

The response of the shah to Saddam's coup (in nationalizing the IPC) was effectively to rekindle the Kurdish revolt in northern Iraq. This time he acted in connivance with Israel and the United States, or at least with Henry Kissinger.

The Shah Plots

The shah concocted his scheme to defeat the Ba'thists in 1970, when Saddam put forward a plan for resolving the decades-old Kurdish problem, a plan that was beneficial to the Kurds, at least as compared to past deals they had been offered.

Barzani (whom we discussed previously) was on the point of accepting Saddam's offer when the shah butted in, so to speak. The Iranian proposed reopening the conflict, through the agency of the Israelis with American backing.

The Israelis would make available weapons seized from the Arabs in the 1973 war; the weapons would be transferred to the Kurds by way of Iran, and America would reimburse Israel for the cost of rearmament, a neat three-way deal—on the surface at least.

In fact, the deal was riven with all sorts of contradictions, which later, when they were exposed, caused complications on a number of fronts.[78] We discuss the outcome of the intrigue in chapter 3. Here we want to look at just one aspect of it, the shah's involvement and how he was able to talk the Americans (or at least Kissinger) into backing such an under-handed arrangement.

Down Days for the Complex

As we indicated previously, thoughout the 1950s and 1960s, the military/ industrial complex in the United States flourished. By 1969, aerospace companies accounted for $120 billion in yearly sales.[79] Seventy-five per-cent of the top one hundred government contractors were in the *Fortune* 500. Of these, twenty-nine made the list's top fifty.[80]

Many of these companies had been in the business for years—companies like McDonnell–Douglas, General Dynamics, General Electric, Lockheed, United Technologies, and Boeing were in this category.[81]

Then there were newcomers not generally associated with the complex— companies like IBM and General Motors; they, too, were getting involved with defense contracting.

Finally, there were some companies that entered the field after having made innovative breakthroughs, such as Honeywell, Litton, Tenneco, FMC, Texas Instruments, and Singer.[82]

All of these companies subcontracted work to smaller outfits. So the web of business interests dealing with the Pentagon was definitely expanding.

Overall, the picture looked extremely rosy; however, it was not that at all. Unfortunately, all of the advances were threatened by developments in Vietnam. In the early 1970s (when the shah was hatching his anti-Iraq intrigue with the Kurds), the war in Vietnam was not going well, to the point that Americans were becoming fed up with it. They were sick to death of hearing Nixon promise to withdraw, only to see him dig himself deeper into what now was popularly being called "the quagmire."

Consequently, elements from within the establishment began targeting the Pentagon, and by association, the complex. In 1971, the U.S. Congress actually went so far as to threaten to cut defense spending for NATO![83] This meant that for the first time in a number of years, the Pentagon was encountering difficulty in funding projects that it had in train. So-called Research and Development (R&D), the mainstay of the military in the United States, and the chief source of subsidies to the complex, was being cut back.

Nixon, of course, was keen to keep up the momentum of defense spending, but he had no grounds on which to mount a case for this. It was then that he and Kissinger conceived the idea of using surrogates in the Cold War, a concept institutionalized in the Nixon Doctrine. Allies of the United States would be asked to take on themselves the job of guarding the "Free World" against communism. The United States would help by providing the military means, but the allies would have to pay for these.

For an ally like the shah this seemed a deal made in heaven. The shah had been buying arms in small increments for years, but now he would be allowed to buy all that he wanted, and the Americans would not hold back anything—he could buy the very latest stuff![84] Of course, all of this was happening before the OPEC Revolution. In 1972, the shah was already spending significant amounts on arms, but this was nothing compared to what he would do once the price of oil shot up.[85]

What the shah reckoned he was getting (in return for these monumental buys) was influence—or, put another way, access not just to the Pentagon but to the White House. He was becoming a seemingly trusted associate of the power elite in the United States.

Most immediately, however, the shah got a spectacular jump in status. Nixon, in a 1972 stopover in Tehran (he was returning to Washington from China), appointed him Policeman of the Persian Gulf. Why the Gulf? Because the British, who until then had been looking out for the area, had decamped in 1969 after admitting they no longer had the economic means to perform this function.

Thus, the shah had acquired a role for himself. This seems to have emboldened him, because right after this he began to intrigue in matters that previously he had kept well away from. He begins to act against the Cartel. Publicly, he raised the old complaint of the oil producers, that he was not getting a good enough deal; gains he thought he had made over the years were being eroded—he said—by changes occurring in the world economy.

Gold

After World War II, America, in effect, kept up the gold standard. Americans were not allowed to purchase gold, but the United States willingly converted dollars into the precious commodity at the London gold pool. This enabled gold to perform what may be considered its primary function, acting as a standard, a gauge against which the health of a nation's (and the world's) economy can be measured.[86]

However, as Lyndon Johnson's Great Society could not support both guns and butter (and because Johnson was determined to continue waging war in Southeast Asia), by 1968 Washington was reduced to combating economic ills by printing dollars.[87] Johnson, and Nixon for a time after him, inflated the American economy.

This had the unexpected effect of driving investors in the United States overseas to buy real estate and to invest in foreign businesses. The Europeans took the dollars earned through these transactions to the gold pool and demanded bullion.[88]

It was not long before a drain on America's gold hoard developed, and Johnson refused to convert.[89] Instead he offered the Europeans bonds. The Germans accepted, and were subsequently burned badly; the French, under Charles De Gaulle, refused.

Because of De Gaulle's intransigence, by 1973, America's dollar pool was seriously depleted, which induced Nixon to restate the value of gold downward. For the oil producers this was a significant step, oil sales being denominated in dollars. Thus, we see the recently created OPEC agitating to rewrite the concessions and the Cartel digging in its heels to keep them as is.

In the period leading to the OPEC Revolution, the producers managed to win a number of oil price hikes. Still, the level remained low, at $3 a barrel. Then in 1973, a concatenation of events triggered an explosion—the famous OPEC Revolution, as a result of which trillions of dollars in wealth was transferred out of Western hands into the coffers of the oil-producing states.

That price hike, which sent the economy of the Free World reeling, by and large was engineered by an odd combination among the oil producers—the shah, the Venezuelans, and Muamar Gadhafi.

Gadhafi

In 1969 the world was surprised by the overthrow of the regime of Libya's King Idriss and its replacement by that of Muamar Gadhafi. Gadhafi, a major at the time of the coup, was an ardent nationalist and adoring of Nasser. Gadhafi and his fellow conspirators, once installed in power, dedicated Libya's oil resources (which were considerable) to the Arab Nationalist cause.

Libyan oil was coveted because, for one thing, it was high grade, but along with that, Libya, being located right across the Mediterranean from Europe, was easily gotten at, which meant that transportation costs could be kept down.

Without going into detail, suffice it to say Gadhafi exploited a weakness in the companies' contract arrangements to whipsaw the Cartel, driving up the price of oil significantly.[90] The companies tried to resist, but because of the way the Libyan concessions had been allotted, they found themselves at the officers' mercy.

Then Gadhafi began to leapfrog in OPEC negotiations. He would insist on negotiating with the oilmen separately from the Gulf producers, wait till the Gulf producers had agreed on a royalty schedule, and then refuse to sign unless he got a better deal than his Gulf colleagues.[91]

To offset that tactic, the Cartel members wanted to negotiate with all of the oil producers at once—no double-teaming. However, because of the Americans' unique situation, to do that they first had to get Nixon's permission.[92] The oilmen thought they had gotten his assent, but evidently they were misled.

The shah seems to have made an end-run, appealing through Nelson Rockefeller to Kissinger. The latter was Nixon's National Security adviser (and later secretary of state, concurrently), but he was also, in a manner of speaking, the Rockefellers' man in government. For years, the shah had been cultivating the Rockefellers through his Chase Manhattan Bank connection, and now he wanted Kissinger to back him (and his fellow OPEC members) against the scheme of the oilmen to nix the double-teaming tactic.

This maneuver he carried out in secret, so the oilmen actually went to Tehran to commence negotiations, not knowing they had been foxed. Once there, however, the shah informed them the old-style negotiating process was still in play (that is, of having two teams operate).[93]

The oilmen immediately appealed to the U.S. ambassador in Tehran, who informed them that Nixon and Kissinger (as the shah was claiming) had agreed to this procedure.

From that point on, the negotiations were a farce. With Gadhafi and the shah *both* leapfrogging, the Cartel was forced to concede a price way above that which it had banked on getting before the negotiations started.

Concurrently with these maneuvers, something else went on that affected the oil industry much more profoundly. The Arabs, who under Nasser's leadership had been a formidable entity internationally, were losing out under his successor Anwar Sadat. The new leader of Egypt was either indisposed or incapable of resuming hostilities against Israel.

In fact, Sadat was merely dissembling. He and his fellow Arab leader, Assad of Syria, had been planning for some time to go on the offensive against the Jewish state, and in line with that, had approached Faisal, king of Saudi Arabia. To the king, Sadat made the argument that time was running out. The Israelis had seized Palestinian lands starting in 1948; this was now 1973, and the world was getting used to the idea of the occupation; it could become de jure.

Sadat wanted Faisal to hold in reserve the oil weapon. Should Sadat and Assad deem it necessary to pressure the Americans (once their planned war had started), Faisal was to threaten to turn off the oil spigot.

We made much earlier on of the antipathy of the traditionalist leaders, like Faisal, for the secular/military men like Sadat. However, Sadat was not your usual military man. He had, for one thing, expelled the

Russians from Egypt, which appealed to the anti-communist Faisal. Along with that, as noted previously, Sadat had been (and perhaps still was) a member of the Muslim Brotherhood, an outfit in which the Saudis reposed infinite trust. So, Faisal assented to Sadat's proposal; he agreed to become an accomplice of the Arab conspiracy.

Having so agreed, Faisal may have gotten cold feet, because he then tried to warn Nixon (through a delegation of top oil executives) that the Arabs were about to launch a war.[94] Faisal wanted Nixon to adopt a more evenhanded approach to the Palestinian question.

The delegation could not get past the deputy secretary of state–level to see the president! Here again one would assume it was Kissinger who was the obstacle. As James Eakins (America's ambassador to Saudi Arabia) wrote after the oil crisis had erupted, "You couldn't get anybody to focus on it [oil]. Everyone thought the price of oil was coming down forever. Everyone thought there was a permanent glut."[95] Frustrated by their rebuff, the oilmen passed their message through the bureaucracy, but of course nothing came of it, and the attack on Israel went ahead.

Once the attack came off, Faisal sent yet another warning to Nixon: there was still time to keep the oil weapon sheathed—if America would just not take Israel's side in the war. Nixon may never have gotten that message either, because the president immediately proclaimed his full support of Israel, and he followed that up by stripping America's arsenals in Europe almost bare to resupply the Israeli army, which, by then, was falling back on both the Egyptian and Syrian fronts.

That left Faisal no option but to declare the Arab oil embargo, in which practically all the Arab countries participated. The embargo was selective in that it targeted just two states—the United States and the Netherlands—but even so it was effective. Within days, the price of oil that formerly had stood at $3 a barrel shot up to $11 a barrel.

At that point the shah, with the backing of the Venezuelans, intervened to, in effect, derange the oil market for good and all. He moved on two fronts. First, he exploited what, to him, was an adventitious occurrence, which is to say the shah had no inkling the embargo was set to come off; it was purely an Arab affair. Nonetheless, the shah and the Venezuelans were able to drive up the oil price as far as it would go, while the Saudis, interestingly, fought to keep it down.

The other front on which the shah moved was the spot market. As we said earlier, he had been selling his increment of independent oil (independent of that produced by the Consortium) on the spot market for some time. When the Arab embargo hit, the OPEC countries were committed to selling their oil through the Cartel. But once the shah started throwing his on to the spot market, where he got $17 a barrel for it (whereas the other OPEC countries were getting, tops $11); the producers, in effect, tore up the concessions, laying claim to all of their oil for themselves. To be sure, they did not immediately deal the Cartel companies out. They initially renegotiated the concessions so the producers could claim slightly higher equity. However, this merely was a stop-gap. Once the producers started to reclaim their oil, they went all the way, and in the end, the Cartel companies became traders for the producers.

Thus, the oil market was turned upside down; the erstwhile underdogs (i.e., the producers) were now the top dogs. They set production schedules, and that meant that any hope of regulating production (so that the price could be fixed in the centers of demand) had ended. Oil would now trade at whatever price the producers chose, for a while anyway.

Immediately after the OPEC Revolution, regulating production was the last thing the producers had to worry about; so panicked were the consumer countries at having to watch the price of oil shoot up, up, up, they grabbed whatever oil was available, against the day when the price would, they felt, go even higher.

In any event, an era had ended, and, as with the Iranian oil nationalization fight, a lot of the blame for what occurred must be assigned to the Americans. They were forewarned of trouble in the Gulf. To dismiss those warnings, as did Nixon and Kissinger, was irresponsible. Oil fueled the recovery of Europe; it was the driver of the whole capitalist system, where it had replaced the erstwhile number one energy source, coal.

How could the United States be so heedless of what was the world's (not the Americans', but the world's) staple industry?

It was bad enough that Nixon and Kissinger had sided with the Israelis in the 1973 war, but to similarly have backed the shah against the American oilmen (over the question of double-teaming) is hard to understand. This delegation, which was going out to Tehran, comprised the top executives in the American oil business.

To be sure, Nixon had his problems. At this time, he was about to come under indictment for Watergate. But, when one looks at the consequences of acting against America's interests on so many fronts, one is struck with the apparent shortsightedness of what the Americans were doing.

In any event, the world was changed now, forever. With energy priced at three times its pre-OPEC value, the economies of the OECD countries (not to mention of the Third World) would have to be reconfigured significantly to accommodate price rises on practically everything.

CHAPTER 3

The Political Effects of the Third Oil Shock

When Britain pulled out of the Gulf in the late 1960s, the United States was unprepared to take over there. Washington had no policy for the area, except as encapsulated in formulaic responses about ensuring access to oil and defending the area against Soviet invasion.

This was not policy. The declarations, high sounding though they may have been, committed Washington to nothing and bore no relation to what Washington was actually doing in the region.[1] During the period we are going to be looking at, Washington mainly was selling arms to the local monarchs. U.S. policymakers apparently did not see a contradiction in this; which was that, if the focus of activity in the area was oil production, the region ought to have been kept stable.[2]

Arms trading promotes wars, and wars are what the United States got. The period from 1972 to the present has been for the area one of almost constant large-scale, bloody conflict.[3]

We begin our discussion of the era of American influence in the Gulf by resuming our narrative of the shah's involvement with the Kurds, which led to war in 1974.[4]

We then discuss the fall of the shah, an event that caught Washington by surprise, and that in itself is remarkable. Given the shah's putative importance to America's professed security scheme, Washington ought to have been alert to the fate that was overtaking its protégé.

Then we discuss America's relations with the other important Gulf States, most notably Iraq. We compare modernization and nationalization under Saddam Hussein with what occurred under the shah, and we will see how the United States related to both experiences.

Finally, we discuss the implications of the revelation, which came to the Americans in 1986, that the Gulf was vital to them, something they may have paid lip service to in the past, but that they never seemed to have comprehended fully.

The End of the Affair

Commentators on Kurdish affairs are prone to ignore the 1970s' involvement of the shah with the Kurds. In this author's view, the affair is significant for what it tells us about Iran and Iraq at a key stage in their development.

The two had come to a significant juncture; this was the case with Iran particularly. Until 1975, the shah had only a single aim (or at least so it would seem)—to ingratiate himself with the Americans. He succeeded in that beyond anything that he probably could have imagined.

Then, in 1973, the OPEC Revolution hit. The price of oil shot up, and the shah (along with everyone else in OPEC) found himself sitting on treasure trove—oil was a trump in everyone's book.

Thus, it must have appeared to the oil producers that they need no longer curry favor of the Americans. Rather, they should break free of trammeling alliances, making themselves autonomous. They would seek to achieve their long-sought goal of realizing a surplus, to spend however they wished.

As of 1975, the shah seems to have undergone such a conversion. He perceived that, with so much money from oil sales, there really was nothing to which he could not aspire. (The Iraqis evidently had a similar perception.)

Why carry on a wasteful feud, which only benefited the Americans (and the Israelis), when the Iranians and Iraqis had better things to do with their money?

It was with something like this in mind that the shah agreed to compose his quarrel with Iraq, a reconciliation brokered at the 1975 OPEC Congress in Algiers. In return, the shah got from Saddam Hussein (the Iraqi who negotiated the deal) a commitment to give up half the Shatt al

Arab, a huge concession for the Iraqis.[5] Saddam got a pledge from the shah to stop meddling with the Kurds.

Overnight the Barzani rebellion collapsed, and the frantic Kurds, to save themselves, spilled over the border into Iran where they took refuge. Bitterness over this sell-out (not just by Iran but by the Israelis and Americans as well) has lingered among the Kurds to the present day.

What the shah had done was extraordinary. Here was an individual who, despite having for the major part of his career been angling to impress Washington, suddenly disassociated himself from a project to which the Americans had committed themselves. This embarrassed Washington, particularly as, at the time that it was done, the Americans could ill afford to be publicly repudiated.

Washington's stature among nations was on the decline. It had lost the Vietnam War, and now it was losing out in the economic sphere as well. Talk was of a new multipolar balance, one that emphasized economics over security and where the United States would have to share power with Germany and Japan.

If Japan and Germany could break into the charmed circle of recognized world leaders, why not Iran? The shah's public statements during this time seem to point to the fact of his aiming to accomplish just that.[6]

The Shah's Fate

The shah wanted to stand among the first rank of the world's rulers, and one could speculate that he might have made it. Certainly with the Iraqi quarrel composed he had nothing to occupy him on the war front.

That the shah failed was due primarily, to two things—one, the state of the world economy, which sabotaged his modernizing efforts, and two, the shah's military relation with the United States, which became an issue and ultimately drove him from his throne.

Put simply, the shah overreached. Perhaps because he was dying (and knew it), he tried to force the pace of modernization.[7] Instead of paying cash for purchases, he started borrowing, with the notion, evidently, that this would enable him to build bigger, faster.[8]

At the same time, the shah lobbied through OPEC to keep up the price of oil, because, in his calculus, the more he got for his production the more he had available to spend. What he overlooked was world economic conditions.

The price of oil, as we know, is instrumental on the inflation front. By keeping the price high, the shah was indirectly helping to inflate the world's economy, and that of course affected the prices of many of the things that he needed at home. Confronted with rising costs on the domestic side, the shah imposed controls. He ordered the *bazaaris* (the middle men supplying goods and services to Iranians) not to raise prices.

However, the mere fact of his ordering it did not mean it was going to work. Iran had acquired a class of *arrivistes*. These were new money men. Interestingly, in a large part, they were made up of the shah's extended family plus high-ranking military officers.

The fortunes of these people were based most notably on the arms deals the Americans were transacting with the shah. For every one of the deals there had to be a commission paid, which went to the middle men who acted as agents for the sale.

These were bribes, pure and simple, but they were a tradition in the arms business. Indeed, the business was so structured that the commissions were, practically speaking, essential.

In any event, the commissions went into the pockets of those closest to the shah, but then, since the courtiers had their clients to maintain, a certain amount trickled down to support these clients.

It was the wheeling and dealing of the new money men that raised complications for the shah when he tried to gain control of Iran's failing economy. With cash in hand, the arrivistes easily importuned the bazaaris into selling them goods they craved, and this, of course, gave rise to a black market. Once that developed, inflation just kept on rising.

Traditionally, the bazaaris and the Shia clergy in Iran are a team; this has to do with the nature of the Shia religion.[9] Suffice it to say, when the bazaaris are unhappy they bond with the clergy, and this explains the heightened mood of religious protest in Iran at the end of the 1970s.

The other piece of this puzzle is the civil servant class, especially hard hit by inflation. Civil servants had to subsist on fixed salaries, which could not be raised because, along with prices, the shah was controlling wages. Therefore, this lot could not pay the black market rate and had to forfeit goods that, in many instances, they had to have.

With the newly rich parading their wealth (which they unwisely did) the poor and underprivileged seethed.

Thus, the bazaaris were being squeezed, and they in turn were squeezing the public, which led to widespread discontent. The clergy castigated the shah, not for his counterproductive economic policies, but for his a-religious program of modernization.

What was wanted, for an explosion to occur, was an issue. This was supplied by the Americans.

Identifying the Enemy

The corruption that was taking over in the Imperial Palace was as apparent to elements in Iranian society as it must have been to the shah. Those perspicacious ones noted Iran's army never fought a war.[10] Yet year after year the shah expended enormous sums on weapons.

To the opponents of the shah, there was a connection between courtiers supplementing their lifestyles with bribes from the American arms dealers and the dysfunctionality of the military (vis à vis war fighting).

To be sure, the opposition saw this as a plot; that is, the imperialist Americans were deliberately suborning the Iranian military to make it a vehicle whereby the Americans could penetrate the country.

This was not precisely so; the Americans had no such scheme. But, ironically, even without their having schemed it, they brought about this result.

We noted earlier that, in the era of the oilmen, the concessions constituted the mechanism whereby foreigners came to exercise control over the Gulf rulers. In the era of American dominance in the Gulf it was now the commissions paid by the arms merchants that performed this function. The recipients of the commissions had a stake in keeping up the American connection, since, as we said earlier, their lifestyles depended on it.[11]

In any event, opposition to the shah came to focus on his military ties to the United States. It was a particularly unfortunate development for the shah, because at that time the American military was practically omnipresent in Iran. It was estimated that there were between 50,000 and 60,000 Americans, mostly U.S. military personnel, acting as trainers for the Iranian military, and arms contractors living in the country.

Under the arrangement worked out between the Pentagon and the shah, these foreigners were regulated by the so-called Status of Forces convention, which specified that Americans who transgressed Iranian law must be tried in American courts.

That issue was what the Iranian mullahs seized on to focus opposition against the shah's rule. The mullahs agitated around it, stoking resentments among the Iranian people, all the while casting their net wider and wider and generating more discontent.

Had the shah been luckier—and had there been a Republican in the White House—he might have weathered the storm. But Jimmy Carter, facing a deteriorating economy at home, was not much interested in foreign policy, least of all in regard to the shah. Indeed, Carter was embarked at this time on a far-reaching policy of cutting arms purchases, which of course formed the shah's principal link to the Americans.

Further, Carter espoused human rights and urged the shah to open his society, something the shah could not do. If he was going to retain his throne he needed to crack down, not open up.

In 1979, the balloon went up, so to speak, and the shah was driven into exile.

Staying Afloat

We noted previously that, under Carter, the military/industrial complex had fallen on hard times. Richard Nixon had begun cutting back on expenses for Vietnam even as the war wound down, and Carter kept on cutting. Given the state of America's economy, there did not appear to be an option; military expenditures could simply not be kept at their previous high level.[12]

The economy, which had steadily improved from the end of World War II, had started falling in the late 1960s, as the strain of funding the Great Society and fighting a war in Southeast Asia proved too much for it.[13]

By the mid 1970s, the United States was off the gold standard and battling to retrench on a number of fronts. Inflation, which, under the circumstances, one would have expected to have gone down, was bearing up, even climbing. This was what subsequently became known as "stagflation," where the economy stalled in the sense of no longer being able to produce jobs, while inflation, for reasons no one could understand, stayed high.

It was Carter's inability to resolve the stagflation problem that cost him a second term. Collins claims that the principle of growth, the driver of administration policy since World War II, was now dysfunctional.[14]

This may have been, but there was more to it than that. Something much more profound was being subverted: Americans' faith in "Keynesianism."

Keynesianism was the philosophy of the New Deal, believed by Americans to be the one sure way to guarantee progress. Now Keynesianism was failing; it could not get America out of its stagflation-engendered slump.

Enter Ronald Reagan. Reagan promoted growth, *with a spin to it*. He put the focus on trimming a "wasteful" bureaucracy and on returning more cash to Americans through hefty tax breaks (supply-side economics, he called it).

On the surface Reagan's policy appeared to make sense—you cut the bureaucracy, that is less to spend on government; you cut taxes and let business invest in growth, this will create new jobs, and ultimately, the economy will turn itself around.

Reagan did something else, however, that was counterproductive for what he was aiming at: he promoted a war against the Evil Empire. He enlisted Americans in a great crusade of defeating the communists once and for all.

Of course, to do that he had to reverse course on defense cutbacks, which he did with a vengeance! In his two terms in office, Reagan spent *over $2 trillion* on arms, the biggest buildup of the military in American history.[15]

One wonders why he felt this to be necessary. After all, we now know that the Soviet Union by this time was moribund—on its last legs, tottering to the dustheap of history, as Marx might have put it.

Why put America so deeply into debt over this matter of defeating communism; was Reagan not beating a dead horse? By the time Reagan ended his two terms, he had tripled the national debt—from $914 billion in 1980 to $2.7 trillion in 1989, a dreadful burden of which the country has yet to rid itself.[16]

To this author, the crusade against communism was specifically to help out the military/industrial complex that, after the down-days of Vietnam, was going through a period of wrenching change brought on by congressionally imposed cutbacks. Further, by making the thing into a crusade (as he did), Reagan bought the support of several key constituencies in the United States, all right-wingers.

The new coalition combined the financial clout of the arms manufacturers with the ideological savvy of mainly former Democrats. The
latter were primarily Jews who believed the Democratic Party had gone
soft on Israel. They approved of the military buildup Reagan was undertaking and hoped that, by joining his crusade, to dispose him toward
the Jewish state. Specifically, they wanted him to supply Israel with more
arms.

This group became known as the neo-conservatives, or neo-cons.[17]
(We are going to have a lot more to say about them in the next chapter.)
They were the ones who first exploited the concept of terror, which, for
all we know, they got from Mubarak and Rabin (see chapter 1). At any
rate, when the Soviet Union collapsed, Reagan's big military buildup
came close to derailing. But the neo-cons were able to save it by sub-
stituting a new threat, namely, that of the (so-called) rogue states of Iran
and Iraq, but particularly Iraq. Iraq was to become America's new nem-
esis in the post–Cold War era.

A Study in Contrasts

Whereas the shah had moved too fast with his modernizing, the Iraqis
had survived by being cautious. The Ba'th was unique among Middle
Eastern political parties in that it was notoriously austere. The Ba'thists
did not buy, except to pay in cash. They did not push consumerist policies. Perhaps most importantly, they did not encourage ostentatious
displays of wealth by arrivistes, even though that class certainly existed.

At a time when Iraq was absorbing dollars because of the spurt in oil
prices, the lifestyle of the average Iraqi stayed pretty much the same. His
(or her) health and welfare needs were taken care of, but, of luxury imports, there were none. The ultra-controlling government refused to live
beyond its means, and, in accord with that, it encouraged a prudent lifestyle among the population at large.

So, unlike Iran, there was no inflation in Iraq and there was no new
class that could excite envy in the population.[18] To travelers, the
country seemed classless. It was dreary; it was grey; it was not a fun place
to be—but it *was* solvent.

The man who turned around this situation of policy-directed austerity
was Saddam Hussein. Having presided over the oil nationalization,

he now stepped forward in 1979 to redirect the country's economic policies.[19] Saddam relaxed the tight import controls. The consumer market began to fill with goods. Iraqis bought things they had not known existed. This won Saddam a measure of popular esteem.

Saddam did something else that increased his standing, although the purport of this has never been understood in the West where it has been grossly misrepresented. In 1979, Saddam instituted a purge in which he executed some twenty-one high-ranking Ba'thists for allegedly plotting against him. The affair was brutal, beyond question.[20] But that it was an exercise in sadistic self-indulgence, as it is has been made out to be in the Western media, is overdrawn.

In the first place, the reason given for the purge, that it frustrated an attempt to deliver Iraq into the hands of the Syrians, has merit. The then-ruler of Iraq, General Baker, was essaying to take the country into a union with Syria. Saddam opposed the move on what ought to be seen as being solid ground. First, the majority of Iraqis were against it.[21] Along with that, allying with Syria would have diverted funds presently being spent on the homefront to the Arab-Israeli battle. We just saw how, in 1975, Saddam and the shah negotiated an end to the shah's Kurdish adventure because, as we said, both men realized they had better things on which to spend their money. Saddam was determined not to get dragged into the quagmire of the Arab-Israeli fight, something that, in the end, could only drain Iraq's resources.

Finally—and most important—by carrying out the purge, he revolutionized party politics in Iraq. We said earlier that the Iraqi Ba'th was a vanguard party. When the party took over in Iraq in 1968 there could not have been more than a few hundred full-time members. Ten years later, the number of full timers had not risen very much higher.[22]

Shortly after he acted, Saddam opened the ranks of the Ba'th Party to public enrollment. Vacancies created by the elimination of top Ba'thists (and of their protégés) were filled with new recruits, who previously would not have stood a chance of becoming members, since the Old Guard would have kept them out.

Elite circulation was sorely needed at this time as the party had taken on aspects of a caste. With younger individuals—men and women—flowing into party ranks, the leadership could hope to exploit that which it had never had—a mass base.[23] Although it cannot be defended on humanitarian grounds, Saddam's action in purging the Ba'th of so many old Ba'thists, from a purely practical standpoint (in respect to what it did to rejuvenate party politics) made sense.

Saddam now had a mass constituency, and with that behind him, he moved aggressively to change the country on a number of fronts.

The Economic Revolution

Using the revenue from oil, which in 1979 had gone through the roof once again (thanks to panic among consumers after the overthrow of the shah), Saddam embarked on a program of turning Iraq into the first successful Arab welfare state.[24] To do this he had to overcome enormous obstacles. For all the years that the Hashemites were in power, and for the years immediately succeeding their downfall, Iraq's advance had been deadlocked. The old Hashemite leadership operated on the trickle-down theory—take care of the latifundiaists and revenue generated by enriching this lot would percolate down through the society, lifting all boats, as we say. That had not worked. In fact, the viciousness of the 1958 revolt is a testimonial to the loathing of the people for the royal family, perceived to have done nothing for the common man.[25]

Qasim, who next took power, tried to alleviate the popular discontent, and succeeded somewhat.[26] But his attempt was frustrated by the low intellectual state of the Iraqis. After years of neglect there were simply not a lot of them who were literate, let alone who could function as technocrats or even as competent bureaucrats.

In that regard, Saddam's modernization plan, as conceived, was quixotic. Having no adequate raw material with which to move the country along, the campaign ought to have foundered. That it did not was a function of the personality of the ruler; Saddam coerced the public into cooperating with his scheme. The literacy campaign is an example of this. Saddam confronted Iraqis with a choice—either learn to read or go to jail (the infamous Abu Ghrayb prison). That approach worked wonders. In fact, the results proved so spectacular that UNESCO awarded Iraq a medal and sent research teams to investigate how the program operated.[27]

It will be a long time before a scholarly, unemotional account of the Ba'th under Saddam can be rendered, as much of what went on during his reign has been sensationalized. We have been treated to serial accounts of Saddam's splendid palaces, of the excesses of his two sons, of the horrors of what went on in Abu Gharyb.

The problem is that much of this was (and indeed is to this day) routine behavior for the Middle East. Assad, Nasser, Mubarak, and even Israel's Sharon. None of these are shining lights in the human rights department. As for Saddam's autocratic tendencies, among Arab rulers there has been an unfortunate propensity for rulers to promote dynasties.

What one would have to do to indict Saddam is to show his excesses were beyond the normal, by Middle Eastern standards. There has been an attempt by the George W. Bush administration to do this by highlighting Saddam's alleged genocidal treatment of the Kurds, an attempt that we do not think can succeed.[28]

All of this aside, the record will have to be set straight eventually, and when it is, Saddam will (we feel) be seen as a nationalist, of the same type as the shah. He was ambitious (as one would expect from the son of a landless peasant), but he was also astute enough to see that with all of Iraq's natural assets (not the least of which, the oil), he could play a historic role.[29]

More specifically, Saddam's distinctive contribution as a nationalist was the way he used the Ba'th Party, to discipline Iraqis, making them assets in his nation-building program. There, he was much like Ataturk, whose great achievement was Turkey's Republican People's Party (RPP).

Saddam ruled Iraq using what he called "party methods," which meant running it like a police state. The party cadres were the police, keeping tabs on and systematically eliminating the constituencies of the ancient regime, mainly the Shia clergy and the big landowners, who were also the tribal leaders. It was not always pretty how they did it, but if Iraq was to move forward, that tie to its feudalist past had to be broken. Indeed, the Ba'thists accomplished in the space of a few years what the Egyptians, for example, have never even tried to do.[30]

It was not just in the sphere of economics that they did this. Saddam and the party lifted the status of women. Nowhere in the Arab world (and certainly not in Egypt) have women matched the gains made in Iraq. There was not a career that was closed to them—doctors, lawyers, politicians—whatever they might take up was open.[31]

It was a policy of the Ba'th, under Saddam, that education up to the university level should be available to all who sought it.[32]

Along with that, the Iraqis' general health benefited, largely as a consequence of improved diets. Marr points out that under the Ba'th, the increase in the annual consumption of food was significant, going from $47.64 in 1958 to over $159 in 1975.[33] Indeed, as of the 1980s, it was widely conceded throughout the Middle East that Iraqis had the highest standard of living in the region (the Israelis included).[34]

Of course all of this was done on oil revenue. It was Iraq's fate to have had an ultra-nationalist regime set on gaining autonomy at just the time when the revolution in world affairs made this a realizable ambition—or so it seemed.[35]

The Transformation

Aburish has this to say about Saddam's modernization effort:

> Saddam wanted contractors to undertake housing projects, companies to build sugar-refining plants which would use sugar beets and dates, industrial concerns to mine phosphates from the huge deposits at Akashat and sulphur from the north, corporations to construct brick-making factories, others with experience in land-reclaiming projects, companies to start up dairy and egg farms, and ones with expertise in building railways, and fertilizer and other chemical plants. It was a wish list of staggering proportions.[36]

As implied by the above, the scope of the undertaking was enormous. It is surprising how much of what was tried actually succeeded. As had been the case with Ataturk, Saddam recognized that it was not enough just to import technical marvels in hope that they would run on unattended, like perpetual motion machines. One had to equip people so they were technologically competent; that meant bringing about a transformation of society. In a manner of speaking, one had to get inside the head of the most benighted peasant to turn him on to modern ways.

Effectively, Saddam proceeded on two tacks. On the one hand, he concentrated on improving education so the average Iraqi could begin to function in the modern world. But along with that he brought in outside experts and installed turnkey projects. Foreign firms were invited, in effect, to drop whole industries down on to the Iraqi landscape. Aburish cites the example of the Zubair fertilizer, steel, and chemical complex at an estimated cost of $45 billion, which, he says, was a "massive undertaking."[37]

Had they been tried elsewhere in the Middle East, these sorts of grandiose schemes—and Saddam loved to operate at the grandiose level—most likely would have invited derision. They impressed Middle Easterners when Iraq did them because area natives knew Iraq had the means to carry them through, not just the money and education, but the discipline—the discipline came from the party.[38]

The Iraqi Ba'th Party was the most disciplined and well organized in the Arab Middle East. Until it came along, there was nothing on the Arab side to compare with Ataturk's RPP. Of course, among the Iranians there has not been an effective political party till this day.

There was one area, however, where the Ba'thists thoroughness and determination was fated to cause problems, mainly with the United States, and that was in the area of armaments. Saddam wanted a competent military, and he recognized that, in today's modern world, this would mean acquiring the latest weapons systems.[39]

Aburish cites a statement of the Iraqi leader to the effect that he (Saddam) recognized that the states that supplied Iraq with arms were friendly but would not always be so. Iraq must therefore (according to Saddam) be prepared to manufacture arms when it is appropriate to do so, even when this conflicted with the strategies of the supplier nations.

Saddam was to act on his perception later (after the Iran-Iraq War) when he tried to build an Arab military/industrial complex. This, as much as anything—we believe—is what led him into the series of escalating clashes with the United States.

Making Friends with the Saudis

In 1979, the United States was not yet thinking about going to war with the Iraqis. Mainly it was concentrating on figuring out a way to survive the disappearance of the shah. The shah's fall, and his replacement by an anti–United States Islamic Republic, left America without a base in the area.

Under the shah, Iran had fulfilled the function of providing a base. Where was the United States to set up now? There were plenty of small

sheikhdoms that would have loved to have become America's basing-
area. But all were too small or too inconveniently located. The only log-
ical candidate was Saudi Arabia.[40] However, as we saw in chapter 1, there
were difficulties with this, difficulties that were tied in with the religious
sensibilities of the Saudi natives.

Actually, as it developed, this was not a problem initially. At this stage
(1979) the United States was not interested in setting up a base for troops;
it wanted to locate surveillance equipment there. Surveillance was one
function Iran had served under the shah; the Americans had set up lis-
tening posts along the Iranian-Russian border to eavesdrop on the latter.

Now the Americans wanted to do the same in Saudi Arabia; they
would make it the base for the AWACS (Airborne Warning and
Control System). That did not require a large military complement to
operate, so in that respect the problem of catering to religious sensibilities was easily finessed.

There was another problem, however, and that involved the suppor-
ters of Israel in the United States; they were bound and determined to
wreck the rapprochement between America and the Saudis. When
Reagan in the 1980s first proposed selling AWACS to Riyadh, AIPAC
(the American Israeli Political Action Committee) mobilized all of its
considerable resources in the United States to scuttle the deal.[41]

It took all of Ronald Reagan's "great communicator" skills in mobilizing public opinion to overcome the furor the Zionists stirred up in the
Congress over this. In the end, he did it, and for a time it appeared that
the United States and Saudi Arabia were moving toward developing a
solid base of cooperation.

Still, there was yet another fly in the ointment, so to speak. There was
one more area sure to generate friction between the Americans and
Saudis—OPEC.

Reagan and Oil

Saudi Arabia, with the advent of the great OPEC Revolution, rode high
as it were. As possessor of the world's largest resources of oil, reserves
that were simple to extract and of the highest grade (and as the country
with the most technologically advanced facilities), Saudi Arabia could

put more of this precious commodity on the market and so reap phenomenal rewards.

Petro dollars flowed to the Saudis' treasury, and naturally, these had to be invested—in the United States (and to a lesser degree in Europe), as the only really secure depositories. This movement of dollars had the effect of firming up ties between the Saudis and Americans long before Reagan fought the fight over AWACS.

At the same time, the Saudis moved on other fronts to draw themselves into a closer relationship with the United States. They began building up their military, as the shah had done by buying American arms. In the beginning, it was not so much arms the Saudis purchased as infrastructure—roads, airfields, and various big-ticket (but nonmilitary) projects.[42]

Gradually the Saudis came round to buying the actual weapons. By the late 1970s, they had replaced the shah as the number one overseas purchaser of American-made arms.[43]

However, there was a contradiction in what the Saudis were doing, and this had to do with oil. OPEC's Revolution had knocked the economies of the industrialized countries off balance, driving up the price of virtually everything. It subjected the world's societies to inflationary pressures, and then, in reaction to that, a form of deflation, or at least recession, set in.[44] A kind of a one–two punch affected the consumer countries, for which the OPEC countries could be blamed.

OPEC, since its creation, was split into a so-called high and low absorbers, a distinction usually lost on the layman. Simply stated, it means that a country with a large population (such as Iran) can absorb lots of cash, and so it is likely to pursue hawkish policies that drive the price of oil up. Conversely, a country like Kuwait, with a low to inconsequential population, cannot absorb much, and it seeks to string out sales over a longer period; to do so it has to keep prices down.

Immediately after the OPEC Revolution, and for a while afterward, the hawks were in the ascendancy. Hawkish Iran and Venezuela fought to push oil prices as high as they could get them. The Saudis and other monarchs of the lower Gulf equally were determined to keep the prices down.

After the shah fell, Saudi Arabia and the lesser sheikhdoms came to the fore. They became what was later to be known as the OPEC Core. Through this group, Riyadh set the policy for OPEC, often over the objection of countries such as Iran, which under Khomeini remained hawkish.

The Saudis attempted to please all parties, hawks included. But given their natural economically derived penchant for moderation, it so happened that they (and the other members of the core group) were on the same wavelength, so to speak, as the Americans and fellow Organization of Economic Development (OECD) countries. As long as demand held up, the Saudis' determination to moderate did no more than cause annoyance among the hawkish OPEC states. However, a crisis developed when, in the early 1980s, the aforementioned recession caused oil sales to fall off appreciably.

Suddenly, OPEC countries, which had gotten used to getting whatever price they demanded for their oil, saw themselves losing out. The downturn hit some countries harder than others. Iran, which was by then fighting a war with Iraq, particularly was hurt. Tehran (under the ayatollahs) had a policy of not borrowing from foreign banks, and therefore needed all the oil revenue it could get.

So, one could say that until the mid-1980s, the Saudis were doing the industrialized countries a favor by holding down the price of oil. Interestingly, the one country that ought to have been grateful—the United States—was not.

America Exposed

Carter, by his high-principled stand on human rights, had undermined the regime of the shah. Reagan similarly came near to wrecking America's link to Riyadh. He did it over OPEC. Reagan opposed OPEC on a number of grounds. He equated it with the oil sheikhs. The caricature of the venal, grasping oil sheikh was to the Americans the symbol of the would-be cartel. Reagan was additionally put off by OPEC's regulatory function; it was so anti–laissez faire (and smacked, most probably in Reagan's mind, of socialism).

Reagan actually publicly declared that he would kill OPEC, given the opportunity, and there are those who believe that he tried to do just that.[45] According to OPEC secretary-general Sheikh Yamani, Reagan conspired against OPEC, and, although Yamani is not specific as to details, he almost certainly refers to the attempt of Britain's Margaret Thatcher to destroy OPEC's pricing schedule in 1985, a move that Reagan applauded and to which he lent support.[46]

After the OPEC Revolution, Britain developed its own native oil industry in the North Sea,[47] and now in 1985, Thatcher repudiated an agreement upheld by the previous Labor government, the effect of which had been to support the OPEC producers' production levels.[48] When warned by OPEC's secretary-general Yamani that this would have unwanted repercussions, Thatcher ignored him.[49]

The suddenness with which events accelerated after that was breathtaking. The Saudis, apparently had been positioning themselves to wage a price war for at least a couple of years. Thus they were ready with a strategy.[50] Once the Saudis unveiled their scheme, companies flocked to do deals with them, and because Riyadh had the most oil and the most up-to-date facilities, it was not long before it had cornered the market.

Producers like the British, which sought to undercut the Saudis' price, lost out. The Saudis could make a profit on volume at the very lowest price; the British—and indeed practically all other producers—could not. So, as the oil price dropped, one by one the other producers went to the wall.[51] The price went from $31.75 a barrel at the end of November 1985 to $10 at the beginning of 1986.[52]

Thatcher came immediately under pressure because the North Sea oil, which is extracted by cumbersome methods from beds thousands of kilometers down, is not nearly as cost-effective to produce as oil from the Gulf (where, as they say, it leaps practically unbidden from the desert sands).

Nonetheless, even as Britain's oil industry came under attack, Thatcher held fast. Reagan, on his end, was delighted. We earlier mentioned the president's big arms buildup and how that had aggravated inflation in the United States. Now, suddenly, with oil prices plummeting, inflation went into reverse. This allowed Reagan to trumpet the success of supply-side economics when, in fact, it was the turnaround in oil prices that had righted the ship.

However, Reagan miscalculated insofar as he failed to look out for the downside. He evidently believed that there was a limit below which the oil price could not go, and that was $10 a barrel. The price hit $10, broke through, and kept plummeting. Reagan awoke to discover that he (or rather Thatcher, who, we must assume, was directing this campaign) had killed the native American oil industry.

Like the North Sea operators, American producers have higher costs than producers elsewhere (and very much higher than those in the Saudi desert); thus they cannot survive when the price goes below $10 a barrel. Once the price broke the $10 barrier, the southwest of the United States began to shut down, so to speak. Not only oil producers went out of business, but oil field equipment manufacturers and even banks that had loaned to the oil producers were liquidated.

The implications of this proved strategically adverse as well. America has always strategized on the basis of its being self-sufficient in oil and of not having to import huge amounts in wartime.[53] Contrast Britain, which was overseas-dependent on oil from the 1920s. Britain's imperial strategy was wholly predicated on preserving a lifeline to the Persian Gulf, which it could only do by committing significant amounts of cash, which Britain's depressed economy couldn't supply, necessitating Britain's pullout of the area.

Now, suddenly the United States was similarly embarrassed. It was about to become a net-importer of oil—a condition that would only worsen. The country's national security strategy was going to have to be overhauled in order to accommodate this new reality.

At the very same time that this awareness intruded on the Americans, they discovered the instrumentality of OPEC in setting world oil prices. They could not kill that organization, as Reagan (and Thatcher) had tried to do because they needed it as a regulator; otherwise, the market would go up and down like a yo-yo, which, for the oil industry (and for any industry with long-term planning needs) was anathema. The regulatory function OPEC performed was, in a manner of thinking, an extension of the cartelization process that obtained prior to 1973. OPEC had never succeeded in becoming a true cartel because it lacked muscle (there was no one to play the enforcer's role, as Britain had done), but it was the next best thing to one.[54] There had to be some institution run along lines of OPEC were the oil industry to be managed efficiently.

Effectively, then, we may say that, as of 1986, the U.S. position vis à vis the Gulf had deteriorated badly. Starting in 1969 with the British announcement that they intended to pull out of the Gulf, things had gone steadily downhill. Immediately after that, the OPEC Revolution hit. Then in 1985, the Saudis ran the price of oil down to where the American oil industry collapsed.

In 1986, the Americans confronted the reality that they depended on the Gulf, not just economically but strategically. Which is to say that, for America, the Gulf was vital.

Damage Control

George H. W. Bush, who was Reagan's vice president at this time, went to the Persian Gulf in April 1986 on what obviously was a damage-control operation.[55] The vice president met with the Saudi ruler Fahd for four days (an extraordinary length of time). At the end of their session, neither man would give a hint as to what had been discussed, except to refer, in what seemed to be purposely vague terms, to the two countries' having reviewed their alliance.

Back in the United States, the media claimed Bush was trying to mend fences in his constituency of the Southwest. A Texan and self-proclaimed oilman, Bush was planning a run for the presidency after Reagan, and he purportedly feared the downturn in the oil industry (in the Southwest) had soured his support at home.[56]

Hence, it was claimed, his trip to the Middle East was entirely on his own initiative; this was disingenuous. Clearly, Reagan had been hoist on his own petard. The great laissez-faire champion, who had openly derided OPEC, was now being forced to acknowledge the importance of the role that OPEC performed.

Reagan had to wrest a concession from the Saudis that they would, in effect, not do this again, that is, set off an oil shock (the third, after 1973 and that which accompanied the shah's overthrow in 1979).

As we said, the details of what Bush concluded with Fahd never have been revealed although there were subsequent leaks in the media.[57] That a deal had been concluded seemed indicated by the subsequent behavior of oil prices. They turned upward again after Bush departed the area, but not the sharp spike upward that the Saudis' fellow OPEC members might have expected. The price went to $17, which was something in the range of what the United States could accommodate.[58]

The Tanker Reflagging

Bush's trip to Riyadh breathed new life into what—thanks to Reagan's ill-judged anti-OPEC campaign—had been a fast-fading relationship. It seems that, in return for Saudi agreement to consult over future oil moves, the Reagan administration (and by extension the Bush administration to come) offered to consolidate existing ties between the two countries.

The test of the reinvigorated relation came in early 1987 when, against the wishes of a formidable array of powerful interests in Washington (and once again most particularly AIPAC), Reagan agreed to reflag the Kuwaiti oil tankers. The decision cost him considerable political capital.

Moreover, the decision was practically sabotaged (or almost so) by a move on the part of the Iraqis. In May 1987, when the debate in the United States over the reflagging waxed hot, an Iraqi aircraft patrolling the Gulf (against the Iranians) fired an Exocet missile that struck the U.S.S. *Stark*, killing thirty-seven crew members.[59] With that, the debate, which as we said had been intensifying, fairly exploded. Against the recriminations of his enemies, Reagan barely survived.

The Iraqis subsequently apologized and agreed to pay an indemnity to the families of the victims. They claimed that it had all been an accident. But was it? Iraq had every reason to oppose the reflagging, as it showed the Americans regarded the Gulf as their sphere. Having accepted that the Gulf was vital to them, the Americans would want to move into the area militarily—the last thing that the Iraqis wanted. Indeed, in the early days of the Iran-Iraq War, Iraq had proposed the formation of a so-called Arab Charter, wherein the riparian states (minus non-Arab Iran) would assume the obligation of defending the Gulf, to the exclusion of the United States.[60]

So, it could be argued that Iraq's attack on the *Stark* was deliberate, a move to tip the balance in the debate over reflagging to Reagan's opponents. If one accepts this interpretation, it would appear that America and Iraq were moving toward a confrontation as early as 1987.

The Iran-Iraq War

It is time to review the history of U.S.-Iraqi relations over the course of the Iran-Iraq War. Actions taken by the United States in relation to the war bore on the clash of the countries later on.

When the war broke out in 1980, the superpowers—United States and Soviet Union—adopted a stance of opposing hostilities. The Soviet Union, Iraq's principal arms supplier, embargoed the flow of weapons to Iraq (the Soviets were never arms-suppliers to the Iranians). It did so, it would appear, out of pique at not having been notified that Iraq was planning to go to war.

The United States refused to supply weapons to either side. However, in this case, the action favored Iraq because Washington, which had been Iran's principal arms supplier, could have agreed to resume deliveries, which would certainly have had an adverse impact on Iraq's chances.

The United States, to be sure, had no reason to support Iran, not after having just suffered through the hostage-taking ordeal. Indications are that the United States, if it did not actively (at this stage) support Iraq, was nonetheless disposed toward it.

For example, it is likely that Washington knew of the Iraqis' intention to invade Iran before the fact. Saddam had traveled to Riyadh in August 1980, where he almost certainly communicated his plans, and the Saudis would certainly have passed on that information to Washington.[61]

Washington probably also assumed that Iraq would overcome Iranian resistance speedily, because the mullahs—as almost their first action on taking power—had gutted the shah's military.[62] Hence, it would have appeared that the Iranians were open and exposed to their enemy.

There is a saying in politics, never invade a revolution. The Iraqis should have heeded that injunction. Their invasion had the effect of suppressing a vicious power struggle going on inside Iran as Iranians banded together to repel the invader. In an astonishing turnabout, that is precisely what they did. By 1982, the Iraqi army had been thrown back across the international border to the gates of Basrah.

The Iraqis held fast outside of Basrah, repelling the Iranians and inflicting enormous casualties on them.[63] Once it became clear that Iraqis were still in the war, the United States dispatched the Democrat, Representative Stephen Solarz, to Baghdad in August 1982 to discuss cooperation between the two countries.[64]

The Iraqis agreed to discontinue support for terrorism (they subsequently expelled a group called May 15); they also declared support for any undertaking the Palestinians might make with Israel. In return for that, Washington committed itself to resuming diplomatic relations with Baghdad (broken in 1967), and to taking additional measures, which were kept secret.

Among the classified portions of the agreement was a pledge to supply Iraq with satellite photos of Iranian dispositions, an enormous help to the Iraqis, who, being outnumbered three-to-one, were hard put to defend a frontier that stretched for many thousands of kilometers. The

United States also agreed to work with the Soviet Union to try to bring about a negotiated end to the war in the United Nations.

With those assurances, the Iraqis settled down to fighting what was essentially a war of static defense. Effectively, they were waiting for the superpowers to compel Iran to go to the negotiating table.

Iraq kept up this essentially trusting attitude until 1986.

Iran-Contra

From 1984, when diplomatic relations resumed, until 1986, the United States gave every appearance of making good on its pledge to work for an acceptable (to the Iraqis) outcome of the war. It did not overtly supply Iraq with arms but it did lobby its allies to embargo weapons to Iran. Implicit in that undertaking was that they supply the Iraqis.

Specifically, on the arms front, Reagan lifted America's objections to France's supplying Iraq with Super-Etandard fighters equipped with Exocet missiles. Once that ban was lifted, Iraq opened the tanker war in the Gulf, which had the affect of pressuring Iran financially (and also led ultimately to the re-flagging).[65]

But of all the supportive moves the United States made, none served the Iraqis so well as its offer of supplying intelligence on Iranian troop dispositions. Then, in 1986, the Iraqis discovered that at the same time the Americans were providing intelligence to them, they were spying on Iraq for the Iranians.

Perverse Behavior

When the United States sent Solarz to Baghdad in 1982 to make a start toward cooperating with Baghdad in ending the war, the move made sense. The United States supposedly was guarding Free World access to oil of the Gulf. The Iran-Iraq War threatened to close the Straits of Hormuz; indeed, the Iranians had made such a threat.

As long as the Iraqis were willing to abide by a peacefully concluded end to the war, it was in the interests of the United States, and of all of the industrialized countries, to give it support. As to those who argue that the United States ought never to have supported Iraq—that is foolish. What would they have had Washington do? Back Iran and open the whole of the Gulf to takeover by the Islamic Republic?

That was why, when Iran-Contra broke in 1985, the shock of perceiving what Reagan had done was so great. By supplying satellite photos to the Iranians of Iraqi troop dispositions, and by selling Iran both Hawk batteries and TOW missiles, the United States had set Iraq up for defeat.[66]

Why did Reagan do it?

To understand that one has to examine the involvement of the Israelis, both with the Reagan administration and with the military/industrial complex.

The Israeli Factor

Israel originated the scheme of supplying arms to the Iranians.[67] Its operatives worked out the details and Israelis who figured prominently in most of the negotiations.

Many explanations of why the Israelis did it have been advanced; most, in this author's view, are specious. The Israelis acted for purely commercial reasons. Over the years, Israel had become one of the Pentagon's foremost conduits for illicit arms-trading in the Third World. The Israelis flogged American-made arms on every continent of the globe, and many of the weapons they traded were from stocks the Americans supplied, ostensibly to keep up Israel's defenses.[68]

We have already drawn the readers' attention to Israel's supply of the Kurds in 1975. In that instance, the arms transferred supposedly were from stores the Israelis had seized from the Arabs in 1973. But the Israelis could never have parted with those weapons were they not sure of having their stores replenished by the Americans.

What this points to is the fact that weapons, like oil, are fungible—it does not matter whence they originate, they are usable by anyone. Moreover, once arms start flowing to one side, the opposing side will want them too, making for more arms buying. The Israeli arms industry was flourishing on sales like those to the Kurds.

It is extraordinary how many conflagrations the Israelis fanned. For example, the war between Ethiopia and Eritrea, and of course Lebanon (which we will have more to say about later) is an outstanding example.

It was not only the Middle East where they operated; they did it all over the world.

Arms sales are a major focus of Pentagon activity, and it goes without saying of the military/industrial complex as well. America produces arms for its own defense, but also (as we have stressed) for the United States, arms production is a way of stimulating the economy. For example, statistics for arms sales during the year 2000 show the United States signed contracts for just under $18.8 billion, or about half of all weapons sold on the world market, with 68 percent of those bought by developing countries.[69]

A lot of America's arms sales are up front—U.S. manufacturers visit the trade fairs where they contract to supply arms to whomever is buying. Over and above this, the United States carries on what are called transfers, where no actual money may change hands, or where there is the appearance of exchange when in fact the "sales" are subsidized.[70]

There is a whole other stratum of arms activity with countries that, for one reason or other, are blacklisted by the United States, but are eager *and able* to pay for weapons. Sales to such rogue states are under the table; that is, on the black market.

Here is where Israel has carved out a niche for itself. Arms embargoed by the U.S. Congress could yet be supplied through the Israeli connection.

That essentially is what was happening with Iran in the Iran-Contra business. After the hostage-taking incident, the U.S. Congress blacklisted Tehran from receiving weapons. This seriously affected the Iranians' war-fighting capabilities, since the shah's army predominantly had been supplied by the United States. It did not take long for Israel to open up a line to Tehran, through which American weapons began to flow—secretly.[71]

All of this was kept covert until the time Iran-Contra was exposed. Of course, once exposed, this was bound to affect the relationship between Washington and Baghdad.

Betrayed

The revelations of the U.S. Congress probing Iran-Contra changed the Iraqis' thinking about their war with Iran. Until 1986, when the story came out, the Iraqis were content to allow the United States—working with the Soviet Union—to broker a nonmilitary solution to the quarrel through the United Nations. Once it was seen how Reagan had behaved—supplying arms to the Iranians, at the same time that he was supposedly aiding Iraq—the Iraqi leadership revised its modus operandi.

Among observers of the war, it was always a wonder that either of the belligerents could use the weapons they were buying, so sophisticated were they. The Iranians never really did learn how to use them. As we said, on taking power, they gutted the shah's military and cashiered (if they did not execute) large numbers of the shah's officers. So they were handicapped where using modern arms was concerned, and they never compensated for that lack.

The Iraqis were another story. They were familiar with modern arms because, under the Ba'thists, they bought so many of them—largely because they were trying to stay ahead in an arms race with the shah. In the process of buying them, they learned how to use them. Moreover, during the war, the Iraqis got a lot of help from the Americans. American military attachés stationed in Baghdad after the United States and Iraq reestablished diplomatic relations developed a kind of mentoring relationship with the Iraqi officers.[72] The latter created study groups where they enlisted the aid of the Americans to critique their military performance, which the Americans did with the aid of U.S. Army field manuals.

In 1986, just before the Iran-Contra scandal broke, the Iraqis had lost the southern city of Al Faw. The Iranians had staged a deception. They made a mock buildup in the north, then knifed across the Shatt al Arab, seizing Iraq's southernmost city.

The loss was devastating to the Iraqis. Until then they had been doing well in the war, almost to the point where one could say they were winning. The loss of a major city to the enemy proved a grievous blow, and something that, some feared, the Iraqis would not be able to sustain.[73]

Then came Iran-Contra, where it was brought out that the Americans had doctored satellite photos supplied to Iraq to make it appear the northern buildup was genuine, and that it had been American-supplied (through the Israelis) Tow missiles and Hawk batteries that had tipped the balance in the fight over Al Faw.[74]

With that revelation the Iraqi leadership was forced to concede that its policy of relying on the Americans was bankrupt. At a Congress of the Ba'th in the summer of 1986, the Iraqi general staff confronted Saddam with the demand they be allowed to take the offensive.[75] If they did this, however, Saddam could not micro-manage the war, which he had been doing until then, and which was the reason the Iraqi army had been held back from performing its best. It is impossible to micro-manage an army once that army has taken the offensive.

No one expected that Saddam would give up his micro-managing role. However, he did just that; he turned over complete direction of the war to the military. The decision was taken in secret, so we have no way of knowing what opposition he encountered from fellow Ba'thists. It is not generally recognized, but under Saddam, the Iraqi Ba'th Party had been led by civilians, making Iraq the only Arab regime where civilians—not military men—held sway. The civilian Ba'thists' unwillingness to trust the military led them to salt the units with commissars to spy on the officers.

Once the decision was made, the Iraqi officers began planning what ultimately must be viewed as the endgame. The last battles of the war, as fought by the Iraqis, were impressive. This was the case with the Karbala battles of 1987 in particular.[76] Of even greater significance was the so-called *Tawakalna Ala Allah* (In God We Trust) campaign of 1988, which effectively brought victory to the Iraqi side.

The success of that campaign came as a great shock to everyone, most particularly to the United States.[77] From the Americans' perspective, the situation that now had come to pass was bad. The balance of power in the region had shifted entirely over to the side of Iraq. Iran's army had just disintegrated. It was not a question of its having retreated, to regroup and return the following year. *It was done.* The show was over. Khomeini was forced, as he put it, to drink the bitter cup of poison (that is, defeat).

Since it had been American policy that there be no military victor in the war (since that would have forced a showdown over America's continued presence in the Gulf), Washington was motivated practically to keep the war going. In that respect, Israel's scheme to supply weapons to the Iranians had had real appeal.[78]

Now, in a manner of speaking, the Americans had been hoist on their own petard. They had committed yet another intelligence failure in a long string of such. What was more extraordinary was that they did not at the time credit what the Iraqis had accomplished. They maintained that the Iraqi army had only won the war by using gas. Implied was that it was not a competent military, that it had somehow cheated. This was a self-delusion on a scale with their refusal to admit in 1953 that they had engineered Mosadeq's overthrow in a coup. Like that earlier affair, they were to pay later for their willful refusal to confront reality.[79]

America's Business

One must have a clear conception of what Americans stand for; what truly is of importance to them? The answer, of course (as we said above), is *business*; Americans are consummate businessmen, and in the matter at hand, what they wanted more than anything was to push arms sales while maintaining access to oil.[80]

How do we know this? Well, look at Iran-Contra, which (in our view) is a dead giveaway. The reader is probably unaware of how many covert arms operations were being carried out under that scheme. They were going on all over the world—the Middle East, South America; the Americans even rang the Sultan of Brunei in on the business. Is it likely that all of this was being done—as the apologists for Reagan would have us believe—because the president could not bear to abandon the Beirut hostages?

It is our belief that the Reagan administration's involvement in Iran-Contra was not at all, or at least not primarily ideological (as it has been made out to be); it was structural. Under Reagan, there had been this tremendous arms buildup, ostensibly to defeat the Evil Empire, but actually, as we have said, to save the military/industrial complex. Now all of these arms, having been produced, needed to be sold, preferably at a profit. Where to?

The Civil War in Lebanon was over; the Iran-Iraq War was about to be, or at least analysts in Washington were fast coming to that conclusion. Perhaps most disturbingly, the Soviets were pulling out of Afghanistan. The only game in town was the Iran-Iraq War. Against the day when that too would be ended, the merchants need to drum up business elsewhere, which meant fomenting new wars in South America, Asia, wherever conditions seemed favorable.

The fact that the Americans would go to these lengths—that is, of trafficking with so many shady characters (such as the Contras) so as to dispose of weapons they had on hand—that says to us that they were desperate.

So, in answer the question posed above (Why did the Americans allow the war to end in a way that was so harmful to their interests?), the answer is: they were not concentrating. All they could see was arms sales; all they were really interested in was arms-trading.

Diplomacy? As we said earlier, the State Department had taken a backseat in this part of the world to the Pentagon. Who in the Pentagon was capable of thinking diplomatically?[81]

Too late the Americans discovered that, by letting their interests slide, they had reaped the whirlwind, or were about to, at any rate.

The Start of the Drift Toward War

Because Washington was so negligent in regard to the Gulf, it was compromised when Iran-Iraq war ended with an Iraqi victory. That brought into play a situation it could not abide; it was not in Washington's interest to see a winner emerge from that conflict, and now that is precisely what had happened.

Faced with what ought to have been seen as a fait accompli, Washington tried to deny the result by, in effect, undoing it, its tactic being to stall the peace talks, which ought to have commenced as soon as Khomeini made his famous speech about drinking from the poisoned chalice.

In the United Nations, Washington backed Tehran's refusal to sit down to face-to-face negotiations with the Iraqis.[82] Since the Iraqis would not budge on this point (that is, their demand for bilateral talks), this meant they could not achieve closure. The situation was suspended.

Also in the United Nations, the United States raised the charge that the Iraqis were attempting to eliminate the Kurds by using gas against them.[83] This was quite a serious accusation (nothing less than genocide) and, therefore, it would appear something that warranted looking into.

At the same time, however, were the Iraqis to have acquiesced to the Americans' demand that the United Nations send a team to the north of Kurdistan, this would have brought about the result that they were trying to avoid; that is, of the peace talks being put on hold. As long as the team was in the north looking into allegations, the Iranians would hold out against having to sit down, and with the United States on the Security Council, the investigation could have been dragged out interminably.

So, Iraq refused to have the U.N. team enter the country, at which point the U.S. Congress intervened.[84] The Senate Foreign Relations Committee sent its own team of staffers to examine conditions in the north, and perhaps not unsurprisingly, the Americans found that indeed the Iraqis were involved in a genocidal attack on their Kurdish minority.

However, the team leader, staffer Peter Galbraith—apparently out of ignorance—overstated the case. He claimed in his report to the committee that, in a two-week period, the Iraqis had gassed and perhaps killed hundreds of thousands of Kurds, something that would have been impossible for the Iraqis to do.[85]

Most Americans seem to be unaware that gas is not a weapon of mass destruction. Army men know this, and so when the staffers made the claim, the U.S. Army challenged it.[86] Of course the Senate Foreign Relations Committee could not rebut the army's assertion, but neither did it admit its validity. Instead, the campaign against Iraq shifted to the media, and here it took a different tack—claiming that the Iraqis were on the point of developing an atom bomb.[87]

All of this, as will be seen, was quite tendentious: the maneuvering of the Americans to demonize the Iraqis by making them out to be a threat, either to their Kurdish minority or to the peace of the world, through their suppositional determination to develop an A-bomb.[88]

Once again, as in the early furor over Rabin and Mubarak's claim of the Iranians leading a jihad against the West, the commotion that was stirred up over this was phenomenal. The turnaround in Iraq's fortunes was such as to take the breath away. One minute Baghdad was America's ally, holding the line against the spread of the Islamic Revolution into the Gulf, the next it was an international outlaw, trying to take over the Gulf by wielding illicitly obtained atomic bombs.

The reader is asked to note the affect of these press campaigns (both this, and the earlier one of Rabin and Mubarak), and to be aware that in this one the neo-cons played a prominent role. At this time, Paul Wolfowitz was serving in the Pentagon as Dick Cheney's assistant, and he was quite active promoting the theory of the Iraqi menace.

What was the aim of all this alarm-raising? The main reason was primarily to get the Congress to vote sanctions against Iraq, as that would make it practically impossible for it to get debt relief.

The Debt Problem

At the end of the war, Iraq faced two imperatives. It had to rebuild its shattered infrastructure, but to do that it first had to pay back debts incurred over the course of the war. These probably totaled around $80 billion, of which $37 billion was owed to its Arab allies, mostly the sheikhdoms, most notably Kuwait and Saudi Arabia.

If Iraq were to satisfy its creditors, it needed time to get its house in order, which is to say that it expected the European creditors to re-schedule. As for debts to the sheikhdoms, Iraq never considered those a problem because in its understanding they were not debts but grants.[89]

In any case, Iraq had but one means of recouping its losses; that is, by selling oil. When the war ended, the price of a barrel of oil stood at $17. Even at that, Iraq would have had difficulty making enough from sales to pay off the interest, which was compounding at a phenomenal rate. Then Kuwait and the UAE started cheating on their quotas, in other words overproducing, thus driving the oil price down.

After the satisfactory (for the Saudis) outcome of the price war with Britain in 1986, Riyadh had announced it would regulate its production to maintain prices in a narrow range of between $14 and $18 a barrel. This represented an effort on the Saudis' part to satisfy the OPEC hawks (who wanted prices as high as they could get them) and the industrial-ized states (who wanted the opposite). This was all very well for most parties, but not for Iraq. If Baghdad were to climb out from under its crushing debt burden, a price of something approaching $25 a barrel was required.

Be that as it may, Iraq had no hope of achieving anything like that. With the UAE and Kuwait cheating as they were, the price could barely be kept from falling below the $17 level. The mystery of course was why these two, Kuwait and the UAE, were doing this. Kuwait had at the time a population of only a few hundred thousand; the UAE less. It would seem they did not need the extra money, and yet here they were selling oil wherever they could, to whomever would buy, and almost at what-ever price they could get for it.

There have been various theories put forth as to why this was hap-pening, and at least one (regarding Kuwait) has some persuasiveness.[90] But figuring out what might have motivated the two is beside the point.

What one wants to ask is, How dare they do it once Iraq indicated its firm disapproval of the practice?

Iraq had just defeated Iran, the erstwhile bogey of the Persian Gulf, the country dedicated to exporting its revolution to the Gulf States, many of which (and most conspicuously this was the case with Kuwait) had large and increasingly restive Shia minorities. Iraq had advertised itself throughout the war as the defender of the Eastern Flank of the Arab World. And now, having won the war, it expected to be rewarded.

Instead, it found itself harassed by the very nations whom the Iraqis believed they had preserved.

In a situation such as this something had to give. In July 1990, Saddam appealed to then-President Bush to use his good offices with the Kuwaitis and the UAE to get them to stop overproducing. Bush, in effect, begged off, claiming that these were sovereign countries and, therefore, he could not interfere.[91]

This was nonsense. The United States interfered all over the world, constantly. As self-proclaimed hegemon, this was the role it had taken for itself.

That it would not move in this area was suspect. Suspicions were added to by Kuwait's subsequent action of announcing that the money it gave Iraq during the war (as a form of relief assistance) was not, as the Iraqis had been led to believe, a grant but actually a loan.

With that, the European banks cancelled negotiations for debt rescheduling. How could they not? The announcement of the Kuwaitis overnight added billions to the amount that Iraq owed.

The Kuwaiti emir's announcement turned Saddam livid, as the emir must have anticipated it would, and yet he made it.[92] Is it likely that he would have done so unless he expected backing from some powerful quarter?

The fact that Saddam, in trying to reconcile the dispute, called in American ambassador April Glaspie and asked her to intercede, would appear to show that, as far as the Iraqis were concerned, it was the Americans who were behind this. Baghdad evidently felt that the Kuwaitis and the UAE, in overproducing on their quotas (and the Kuwaitis in restating Iraq's wartime-obligation), were either (a) colluding with the United States, or (b) taking advantage of Iraq's predicament, knowing that Washington would not object.

In this author's view, it was a combination of both. The American economy had been on a roller coaster since 1973. In 1980, when Reagan came into office, it was in appallingly bad shape. Inflation was killing it, and Reagan's supply-side economic policies had not worked to pull it out of the hole. Indeed, as we pointed out, they could not, not as long as the president pursued his great arms build-up. Consequently, the United States, under Reagan, had run up this previously mentioned enormous deficit.

Bush inherited the distressed economy. Now, just before the first Gulf War erupted, the country was moving into a recession.

So, one could argue that the depressed oil market (with the result of keeping oil prices down) suited Washington, and since, along with everything else, it complicated Iraq's recovery, from Washington's standpoint, that too was a plus.

But the problem was that Iraq needed immediate relief. So burdensome was its debt load that, given the way the interest was compounding, unless relief came quickly, Baghdad would simply have to succumb; it could never climb out. So, when Bush tried to mollify the Iraqis with soothing words (which is what he did, essentially), counseling them to wait, that things would work out, he was kidding himself—but he was not kidding Saddam.[93] Saddam had delivered an ultimatum: either Washington got Kuwait and the UAE to stop overproducing (and Kuwait to repudiate the debt), or Iraq would take unspecified action.

Bush called the Iraqi leader's bluff by persisting in doing nothing, and so America was again surprised when Iraqi forces, in a space of not much more than forty-eight hours, invaded Kuwait and completely took it over.[94]

Why?

Viewed thusly, this whole affair is practically a comedy of errors, at least on the Americans' part. Caught asleep at the switch, so to speak, they find themselves facing a situation they cannot—*will not* abide. To undo it, they enter into a series of transactions that presumably they believe will succeed. However, when they do not, rather than reflect on where their machinations are leading, they redouble efforts to pressure Iraq, and in the end, they provoke a horrendous crisis.

Why could they not have moved slowly, felt their way through this, instead of (as they did) piling one overreaction on to another?

Setting aside ignorance (and the Americans certainly were ignorant of Iraq), something malign was at work—the British and the Israelis were counseling the Americans to take a hard line, and they did it for their self-interested reasons.

Once Iraq invaded Kuwait, Britain as much as the United States found itself compromised. Kuwait was Britain's client. Kuwait banked in Britain, where it dealt in sterling. It also bought arms from Britain, and Britain was a stakeholder in the Kuwait Oil Company.

As soon as the invasion occurred, the British (in the person of Margaret Thatcher) importuned Bush to go to war. In effect, the British were trying to get the Americans to save their bacon. As Kuwait's patron, London ought to have acted to repel the invasion. Since it did not have the power, it pushed the Americans to take on that job.

Israel, even more than Britain, felt itself endangered, not so much by the invasion as by the outcome of the Iran-Iraq War. It was not so much that Israel, militarily, could not stand up to Iraq. What the Israelis feared was a broader realignment of forces in the Middle East.

What Iraq's emergence as a victor in the war portended was a revival of Arab Nationalism, a potent movement as long as Nasser was alive but one that went into decline as soon as he died.

Saddam was an Arab Nationalist, or at least he had recently shown a penchant for playing that card. He had swung round to championing the cause of the Palestinians. He had announced his intention of forming an Arab trade bloc with Jordan, Yemen, and Egypt, and he aimed to create an Arab military/industrial complex with Saudi Arabia and Egypt.

Probably most disturbing of all was Saddam Hussein's intent of unsheathing the Arab oil weapon. His determination to discipline Kuwait and UAE for cheating on their quotas implied that.[95] If we assume—and we think this is legitimate—that the Kuwaitis and UAE were colluding with the Americans to keep oil prices low, then Saddam, by determining to put an end to the practice, was posing a direct challenge to America's professed hegemony.[96]

Had he succeeded in the course on which he was proposing to embark, he might have turned the Arabs into a force internationally. A strong Arab state, militarily confident and strategically positioned inside the Gulf could easily have made its influence felt on world oil markets.

Indeed, one can carry the argument further and say that ultimately what the Iraqis were proposing would have affected all of the producers, not just the Arabs—countries like Venezuela and Iran (the high absorbers) would certainly have gone along with Saddam's plan of pushing for higher prices.

There was already movement toward just this end. After the Iran-Iraq War concluded, Tehran made the unlikely move of publicly supporting a call by Iraq for a price rise, which had the effect of aligning the two on oil policy.[97] To everyone's surprise, Saudi Arabia joined with them. As previously mentioned, Saudi Arabia, after 1973 and the OPEC Revolution, had initiated a campaign to enlarge its population. That campaign had succeeded beyond what anyone would have imagined, raising the figure to somewhere around 9 million. Thus, the Saudis had become high absorbers. With a growing population, they now had a need for more revenue.

A lineup of Iraq, Iran, and Saudi Arabia within OPEC was formidable, or it would have been had Iraq been able to recoup its military strength.

For Israel (and the Americans), all of these indicators of change were not reassuring. Israel, no less than the United States was in a position to do something about it.

If one looks closely at the character of the campaigns against Iraq waged both in the Congress and in the American media, the imprint of AIPAC is all over both. In the Congress, the usual suspects, that is, friends of Israel, led the move to get sanctions imposed on Iraq for the alleged gassing.[98] In the media, a similar lot of stalwarts (people like William Safire and Charles Krauthammer) pushed Congress to take action on the issue.

At the same time, there is no indication Israel or its friends in the United States wanted to push America into war. It seems more likely they would have been content to affect the sanctions, since that would have virtually strangled Iraq, preventing it from winning debt relief.

Still, war was not something to which the Israelis were adverse, and once they and their friends in the United States perceived that through agitation war could be instigated, well, darned if they did not try it again. They moved (as we shall see) to employ techniques developed in the first go-round to maneuver the United States into two more subsequent wars—the one against Afghanistan and the second war against Iraq.

CHAPTER 4

Techno War in the Gulf

In this chapter we look at the first war of the United States against Iraq. We will pay special attention to the manner in which the Americans prosecuted it. The fight was particularly brutal in the amount of aggression perpetrated against civilians. Civilian casualties in the war were enormous, and that was because of the prolonged bombing from the air carried out by the Americans against Iraqi cities.

America defended its role in carrying the war to Iraq's homefront, but, as we will show, the arguments it used were sophistical. In essaying to punish the Iraqis, Americans deliberately laid aside restraint, turning their backs on the norms of civilized conduct enshrined under international law.

Moreover, when the war ended, America continued oppressing the Iraqi people through its Dual Containment policy, which manipulated U.N. sanctions. We will show that this harsh penalization of a whole people provoked a backlash against America throughout not just the Gulf but in all of the Middle East, and beyond.

When the Clinton era ended, America's standing in the region had sunk probably to its nadir.

Targeting Civilians

Americans' conduct of the first Gulf War has been criticized on grounds that they need not have visited such destruction on a third-rate power such as Iraq. It is a matter of record that tactics employed against the Iraqis were designed originally for use against the Russian superpower.[1]

So, it would appear that, under the circumstances, the response against Iraq was excessive.

Why could not the United States have tailored its assault to suit the fact of its having to fight a practically defenseless foe?[2]

American commanders offered justifications for what was done, and we will deal with these. The defenses seem, to this author, to be legitimate in some regards.

At the same time, we will note the behavior of the neo-cons, whom we mentioned in the last chapter. There was pressure on the commanders from these people to press America's enemies hard, to make them suffer. It appears that the Iraqis were the victims of a neo-con- and U.S. Air Force-devised strategy the success of which depended on achieving results in a way that guaranteed the war would be fought atrociously.

The First Iraq War

For the United States, the first Gulf War, if it was not a cakewalk precisely, was almost that. After Washington recovered from the shock of the Iraqi invasion of Kuwait—that is to say, defied America's injunction not to pursue such a course—it set about to reverse the coup, if not to bring down Saddam Hussein.

The biggest part of the operation, for the Americans, was the staging effort: they had to move some 325,000 troops and immense amounts of equipment to the theater. Coinciding with this vast deployment was the diplomatic endeavor of putting together a coalition to oppose the Iraqis.[3]

America could have mounted a one-off operation; in effect have responded to the invasion with bombing raids and such, but as Colin Powell, then Chairman of the Joint Chiefs, opined, "If someone wants to fight with [the United States], then don't play around: kick butt."[4]

There should be no doubt about the Americans' resolve. They intended to return the situation in the Gulf to what it was before the invasion. At the same time, the Americans did not act precipitously; they took their time about it. From the day the war was declared (August 2, 1990) and America started moving forces overseas, to the initiation of combat (January 17, 1991) occupied 136 days.

A number of factors could have led the Americans to adopt such a slow pace. Most notably, the United States was now the sole surviving superpower after the collapse of the Soviet Union. This being the case, Washington did not have to worry about interference from the Kremlin.

It is more likely, however, that the Americans—in as much as they were not prepared for Iraq's invasion—could not get to the theater any faster, at least they could not if they meant to fight a traditional-style war, relying on heavy use of ground forces.

There were those who felt that by taking so long the United States gave openings to the Iraqis to conquer Saudi Arabia. This never was a danger, as, had the Iraqis intended to attack into the peninsula, they would have deployed many more troops than they did.[5]

Iraq wanted Kuwait as a bargaining chip to get out from under its debt load. In four separate communiqués (one on August 12, 1990, another August 19, 1990, one dated September 17, 1990, and finally on September 30, 1990), Saddam indicated this.

Had the United States accepted Iraq's demands (particularly one supposed to have been tendered informally in early August in a letter to Bush from Saddam), the Iraqis could then have retired from Kuwait and counted themselves satisfied. They could have gotten on with their number-one priority of rebuilding their war-ravaged economy. They also would have had Bubiyan and Warbah islands, plus a small stretch of Kuwait along the border, which would have enabled them to begin dredging the Khor Abdullah channel, opening it to deep-draft shipping. With all of this, the Iraqis would actually have been somewhat ahead of the game, having achieved several of their aims of their eight-year long war with Iran.[6]

However, if that was what Saddam had in mind (that he could use Kuwait as a bargaining chip), he miscalculated. Once the United States had determined to oppose the invasion, it seems to have resolved on making war, with the result that all of the Iraqis' maneuvers to initiate negotiations went unheeded.

Negotiations were not on for other reasons. As soon as the crisis developed, various small-fry, seeing an opportunity for aggrandizement, leaped to exploit the situation. This complicated affairs, making it virtually impossible for the United States to deviate from a course of exacting retribution.

The most forward of the opportunists was Egypt. Mubarak's behavior was confounding all along the line. By his maneuvering he kept the crisis boiling; had he left it alone, it might have died down. Evidence of Mubarak's duplicity toward his erstwhile Iraqi ally is supplied by Aburish, who describes how the Egyptian sabotaged reconciliation between the principals. According to Aburish, Saddam had agreed to attend a meeting along with Mubarak, King Fahd, King Hussein of Jordan, and the Emir of Kuwait on condition that the Arabs not attack him verbally. No sooner was the meeting laid on than Mubarak denounced Iraq's invasion, with the result the meeting was aborted.[7]

Ultimately, Mubarak was able to wangle $6.8 billion in debt-forgiveness out of the Americans for his "aid" in repelling the invasion.[8] Mubarak was shrewd in recognizing the degree to which America was dependent on him. The coalition Washington was assembling needed Egypt to take the onus off unpalatable aspects of the affair. Saddam claimed that, in standing up to the United States, he was championing the Arab cause. The Egyptians, by coming over to the United Nations, made that argument untenable.

Mubarak was also influential in securing an Arab League vote against the Iraqis. To do so, he and the Saudis had to amend League voting procedures, which, had they not done so, a pro-Coalition stance could never have been adopted.[9] After the league acted, negotiations between Iraq and the Coalition were a dead letter.

The Egyptian leader was able to exploit the situation further vis à vis the Saudis. What troubled the latter (and we have already discussed this) was the fact of their having to invite American troops into the peninsula. As we said, the presence of foreigners (non-Muslims) in the area of the Holy Places is *haram*. If the Egyptians agreed to accompany the Americans and the rest of the Coalition forces, it was hoped that this would offset native Saudi anger over Fahd's decision to let the Americans into the country. As we have already seen, this proved wishful thinking.

In any event, the Egyptians did well off of the invasion, as did the Turks (initially),[10] the Russians, and a whole host of nations that signed on to the Coalition. By the time the war was launched, the number of opponents was few. In a U.N. vote on August 9 condemning the invasion, only Yemen and Cuba stood out against the Americans.[11] Even Syria joined the Coalition (probably one of the really foolish moves Assad, whose reputation was that of a fox, made in his career).[12]

Why?

Between August 2 (when Iraq invaded) and January 17, 1991 (when the actual shooting war began), Saddam made several attempts to justify his aggression. On August 12, he offered publicly to withdraw if the world community would guarantee Israel's withdrawal from the Occupied Territories.[13] This coupling was calculated to appeal to the Arab street. Indeed, it did appeal—to an extent. The Palestinians were joyous, conducting wild demonstrations in the territories and Jordan, which promptly undercut whatever store of goodwill Arafat had built up with the Gulf sheikhs. To the Palestinians, Saddam's linking of the two previously disjointed issues was a long overdue move. It is likely that many non-Palestinians among the Arabs shared this view. At the same time, however, it is remarkable how dilatorily the Arab street performed in responding to Saddam's appeals. Initially there were a few demonstrations. Later these increased, especially after Saddam fired scuds into Israel.[14] Overall, however, the mob-factor (if we can call it that) never really came into play.

There is a simple explanation for this. All of the Arab governments are repressive, all have powerful security apparatuses to keep the street in check, and these mechanisms were active from the moment the crisis materialized.

Gyring Escalations

One hundred and five days after the Iraqis invaded Kuwait and four days after America's national elections, President George Bush announced he was increasing America's military commitment; he doubled America's troop strength for the Coalition.[15] Thus began the gyring escalation between Saddam and Bush as each strove to gain an advantage by overwhelming the other's deployment.

By pushing up America's commitment, Bush seemed early on to be tipping his hand. Initially he had said that the United States would defend Saudi Arabia because, as he made it out to be, Iraq intended to invade it as well. Nothing was said by him—initially—of winning back Kuwait from the Iraqis.

There was considerable unease in the United States at the outset of the crisis about getting *too* involved. In the view of many Americans,

Kuwait was not worth worrying about. At least one poll (taken August 22) showed 78 percent of Americans opposed a first strike against Iraq, although roughly the same percentage approved of Bush's sending troops to the Gulf.[16] Bush seemed to play on this ambivalence. If he was not signaling determination to fight, he was, by his steady troop buildup, positioning himself so that, if it came to that, he could fight.

Ultimately, Bush notched up the American commitment to an impressive 325,000 troops. But the Iraqis easily bested that with a force of 530,000 troops in Kuwait.[17] Iraq was advantaged in this exchange insofar as it already had a large force under arms (after the Iran-Iraq War). If anything, the necessity of deploying forces was a godsend for the Iraqi leader, who—with his economy falling apart—could not afford to demobilize as he had no jobs to send his troops home to.

Bush not only had to mobilize and dispatch overseas the so-called volunteer army (i.e., the regular force), he also had to call up the reserves, more than 1,040 units with more than 140,000 personnel.[18]

Considerable diplomatic activity went on; several nations offered peace plans. Some of this activity was bogus, making a show of seeking peace while behind the scenes working to close the trap on the Iraqis.[19] In other instances the attempts appear to have been genuine. The Russians made several good-faith efforts to mediate. The problem with them was that their economy was shot; Russia could not afford to offend a country it hoped later on would help extricate it from its debt burden.

Britain seems to have urged a confrontation from the first, and indeed, Margaret Thatcher later boasted she "put fire in Bush's belly," meaning apparently that she exhorted him to stand firm when he might have let down. In this author's view, there was little likelihood of that.[20] Britain's bellicose stand was not without self-interest. As we discussed earlier, Kuwait was, after a fashion, a British client.

France joined the Coalition, but less wholeheartedly than Britain. Under then-President François Mitterand, France sought to make a case for negotiations. Paris had strong economic ties to Baghdad. It was owed over $7 billion for arms delivered during the Iran-Iraq War and had obtained potentially lucrative oil concessions from the Iraqis that it stood to forfeit in the event of a war.[21]

At first, the stand of the U.S. Congress on the war was not supportive. Bush had his work cut out for him convincing Americans, through their

Congress, that a war to defend Kuwait, a country of oil sheikhs, was acceptable. The fact that he had to resort to demonizing Saddam shows how difficult he found this.[22] Americans (as the reader has been made aware) are not partial to the sheikhs. Yet, here was Bush expending considerable effort to defend one such outfit (the Saudis), while he appealed for additional aid to win back territory taken from another.

Actually, as it turned out, America paid virtually nothing for the war. Practically everything came out of the pockets of the Saudis, the Kuwaitis, and the UAE, plus the Germans and the Japanese.

Even so, Americans chaffed over the unwillingness of the Germans and Japanese to send troops. Objections over the refusal were forthcoming in particular from the so-called isolationist camp. This designation of isolationist vs. multinationalist is misleading; it does not reflect the true division at the center of power. In the White House, the split was between those who did not want to fight as long as anything could be gained through negotiations (James Baker and Brent Scowcroft fell into this category) and those who felt anything short of inflicting a great defeat on Iraq was unacceptable (the neo-cons clustered around Dick Cheney in this one).

In the contest between the pro-war faction and those opposed, inertia seems to have played a great role. Bush, who was on the fence early in the war, slowly was pushed into backing the hawks by the facts on the ground as it were. Not wanting to concede to Saddam that he *would not* fight because he *could not* (not having enough troops in-theater), Bush kept increasing the troop level, and as the force got bigger and bigger, he progressively backed himself into a corner. After building up this enormous military presence, Bush could not simply retreat.

The troops in-theater constituted a coercive element, of a sort. As the weeks slipped by and the force kept building and building, the troops (particularly this was the case with the reservists) began to grow restive, wanting to get the thing over with; fish or cut bait, was the sentiment Baker heard on his initial tour of the theater.[23]

Initially, the CENTCOM commander, General Norman Schwartz-kopf's plan was for a ground campaign that was much more elaborate, more prolonged, and potentially more costly (in American lives) than was finally the case. It was divided into two phases—an air war to soften up the Iraqis, followed by a ground war phase. In this first softening-up operation, the air force would concentrate on destroying Iraq's command

and control, and only when the United States could claim mastery of the sky over Iraq, would America's ground forces engage.

It was assumed originally that the air war phase could be gotten through quickly. In fact, the air war went on much longer than anticipated, lasting almost six weeks, during which the air force flew over 88,000 sorties. It was the largest, most devastating air assault ever conducted. Indeed, the United States dropped more bombs on Iraq during this brief period than on Germany during all of World War II. The ground phase lasted just four days.

What seems to have brought about this change was Iraq's defiance. The Iraqis certainly knew that, once the Coalition started building and once they started losing motion after motion in the United Nations, they were doomed; they were stuck in Kuwait. Yet they did not surrender. Such behavior was extraordinary, particularly as far as the regular army troops were concerned.

Iraq's army was constituted into an elite corps, the so-called Republican Guard, and the regulars.[24] The Republican Guard was Saddam's ace in the hole, units whose loyalty he felt was beyond question; Saddam believed that he could depend on them no matter what. Accordingly, he treated the Guard with extreme favoritism.

The situation of the regulars was more problematic. They got few perks—in the form of superior arms, that sort of thing. Moreover, in the deployment, they occupied the front line trenches (the second and third lines as well), while the Guards held a roving commission, circulating behind the lines. The Guards were free agents, and it was this, ultimately, that saved them.

It was not until the ground war began and the Iraqis were subjected to the devastating impact of the American-styled air-land battle that units began decomposing; they surrendered in droves.[25]

The composition of Iraq's forces certainly influenced the strategy the United States adopted. The U.S. Army saw the Republican Guard as the enemy's center of gravity and wanted to concentrate on it, destroying it first, and then—as the army men viewed it—the situation would be resolved quickly in America's favor.[26]

The U.S. Air Force envisaged Saddam and his entourage—the RCC, Saddam's family, the top bureaucrats—as the center and wanted to go after them.[27]

The army lost out in this contest. Emphasis definitely was on Saddam, and that accounts for the extraordinary prolongation of the air campaign.

It probably accounts also for the ability of the American army to over-whelm Iraq's defenses so thoroughly in the end.

The Iraqi army was demoralized by the time the air war phase ended. Nothing so depresses front line troops as awareness the enemy is tar-geting their families and loved ones behind the lines.

By late January the United States had destroyed Iraq's command and control. Because Americans dominated the skies over Baghdad, Iraqi defense against further air attack was impossible.

At a certain point, which the author would put on or about January 25, 1991, Saddam, figuratively speaking, packed it in. This was when he ordered an element of his air force to fly to Iran, seeking safety there against the destructive air raids of the Americans.[28]

After ordering the planes to seek a safe haven, Saddam commanded the army to stop extending its defense line to the west. Schwartzkopf was preparing his so-called Hail Mary strategy of making an end-run into Iraq. To accomplish this, Schwartzkopf had been extending his line far-ther and farther into the Neutral Quarter. The Iraqis had been keeping pace, until abruptly they quit doing so.[29]

It was at this point, we must assume, that Saddam began preparing for the endgame, a strategy that entailed withdrawal of the Republican Guard back into Iraq, while the regulars were left more or less to fend for themselves.

The Model

The first Gulf War has become a template for subsequent American military actions, which is extraordinary. The war came so suddenly it could not have been prepared for. In fact, America's Gulf War strategy grew out of the Cold War. The Americans had discovered during war games that they could not repel an invasion of Europe where Russia could exploit its manpower advantage.

Thus, they devised what they called air-land battle to cope with this problem of overcoming Russia's numerical superiority.[30] Simply stated, the strategy involved bombing behind lines, the idea being to reduce the effectiveness of support units so they cannot move up, or else arrive in such condition (having been torn apart by aerial bombing) that they are, for all purposes, dysfunctional.

In the Iraqi case, the strategy was massaged, so to speak, by air-war theorists who virtually abstracted the land component out of the equation. It devolved into a situation of bombing the Iraqi homefront into submission. The strategy that won for the Americans, reduced to essentials, came down to the air force terrorizing civilians.[31]

The Air War Strategy

General Michael Dugan, U.S. Air Force Chief of Staff, gave a famous (or perhaps one should say, unfortunate) interview to the press days before the war began. In it he revealed that, in the coming war, "downtown Baghdad" would be the "cutting edge" of any U.S. attack.[32]

This created a furor in Washington, as the administration was not looking to tip its hand. Over and above such considerations, something else upset the officials. The general made reference in the interview to the Israelis. He said they had advised him that Baghdad ought to be the focus of U.S. violence. The Americans should target "Saddam's family, his personal guards and his mistress."[33] This particularly embarrassed the Bush administration, which was trying to induce the Arabs to join the Coalition. Any hint the United States would pursue tactics ostensibly originated by Israel (to go after *Arab* Iraqis) was unfortunate, to say the least. Washington sacked Dugan, but then in actual combat, it pretty much proved out everything the general said.

This is the basis of our claim that elements within the Pentagon (namely, the neo-cons) were disposed to fight a new kind of war against the Iraqis, and this departure was associated with the Israelis. We will have more to say about this later.

The carnage brought on by air war strategy was terrible. In sheer numbers of sorties, the scale of the Americans' offensive is hard to grasp: 88,000 raids. Even if only half of those were actual bombing runs, this implies a lot of casualties, and since—as we have just said—the aim was to bring the war to downtown Baghdad. Thousands of civilians must have died.[34]

The Americans studiously refrained from estimating Iraqi losses—military as well as civilian—claiming they had no basis for making a realistic tally. In fact, they almost certainly sought to play down this aspect of the war as it was embarrassing.

From the Iraqis, statistics were also not forthcoming, but for a different reason. The regime was striving to keep up morale and sought to perpetuate the myth of the Iraqis having a hope of survival, if not coming out a victor.

Hiro suggests that if one were to figure at least two persons died as a result of every sortie (and taking into account that only half the sorties were bombing runs), then a figure approaching 100,000 deaths is possible. That seems excessive, but certainly many, many civilians died.

In any event, it is hard to see how Schwartzkopf's denial that "we [the Americans] are not, not, not, not, not deliberately targeting civilian casualties [sic], and we never will. We are an ethical and moral people," can be believed.[35]

After the war Iraq was devastated. Its electric grid was destroyed, its bridges (thirty-seven of them) were down, its major highways cratered, and its water supplies practically cut off to all the major cities. This kind of destruction could not have been accomplished if the Coalition had scrupulously, as claimed, strove to avoid civilian casualties.

Among the Arabs, King Hussein of Jordan was the most outspoken in attacking the "barbarity" of what the Americans were doing. On February 6, 1991, he said "[the United States intended] to destroy all the achievements of the Iraqis and return [Iraq] to primitive life using the latest technology of destruction."[36]

An American, who early took Iraq's side and visited the country on more than one occasion while the fight was going on, Ramsey Clark said on February 12, 1991,

> in all areas we visited and all other areas reported to us, municipal water processing plants, pumping stations, and even reservoirs have been bombed. Electric generators have been destroyed. Refineries and oil and gasoline facilities and filling stations have been attacked. Telephone exchange buildings, TV and radio stations, and some radio-telephone relay stations and towers, damaged or destroyed. Many highways, roads, bridges, bus stations, schools, mosques and churches, cultural sites and hospitals have been damaged.[37]

In our view, no basis exists for the Americans' contention that they fought a "civilized" war in which they strove to avoid harming civilians. It was one of the most—if not the most—brutal wars in history.

Yet, the brutality barely was conveyed to the world at large. A big part of the reason for this was the U.S. military command in-theater censored press dispatches.[38] Consequently, it was only toward the end of the war, when the Iraqi leadership reversed course and allowed Western journalists to tour the country, that the carnage became known.

For example, when the Americans bombed a plant producing baby formula outside of Baghdad, they said it was a chemical weapons factory. Then the Iraqis brought Western journalists to the site where they reported seeing infant formula strewn about.[39]

The journalists also were permitted to inspect U.S. strikes that miscarried, for example, one that leveled a wide swath of the Haifa Street residential and business district, next to government office buildings, which the Americans had targeted. The Iraqis showed off some fifteen houses and over one hundred shops demolished by the bombers.[40]

Perhaps the bloodiest documented assault on civilians was the bombing of an air raid shelter in the Amariya district of Baghdad on February 9, 1991; three hundred civilians perished. The Iraqis laid out the bodies in the street and invited the press to photograph them.[41]

And still, the American disputed the Iraqis' claim, saying the bunker was used by *families* of Ba'thist officials, as if it were all right to kill civilian relatives of the leadership.

This strike on the bunker caused a widespread hostile reaction among Arabs; Jordan's King Hussein proclaimed a three-day period of mourning.

All of this was occurring on the homefront. Iraq's army (being largely committed in Kuwait) was relatively spared. This situation did not last. The Americans eventually brought in some truly lethal weapons, such as fuel air explosives, on a par—in scale of destructiveness—with small atomic bombs.

Then, of course, there was the "highway of death" episode. When the American counterthrust into Iraq finally was launched, the Iraqis, driven into the open, simply were mowed down. On the retreat from Kuwait, the U.S. Air Force killed indeterminate numbers of Iraqi soldiers who, it was later brought out, were in headlong retreat along a six-lane road from Kuwait City. Another reported "massacre" involved the 24th Infantry Division, whose commander, General Barry McCaffrey, was accused (apparently by some of his fellow officers) of war crimes connected with deaths of hundreds of Iraqis who were similarly trying to flee.[42]

In the end, it is probably no exaggeration to say the Americans took a country (Iraq) well advanced into the industrial age and bombed it into what practically was a preindustrial state.

Nor was that the end of it. Because of the destruction of Iraq's infrastructure, disease became rampant after the war. The half a million Iraqi children lost to various diseases during the ensuing sanctions period can be attributed to this.[43]

This then is the gist of criticism of the Americans' operation: the United States took a style of war meant to be used against the *army* of a fellow superpower (Russia) and turned it against a third-rate power, shifting the focus to the Iraqis' homefront.

Reasons Why

There are a number of reasons why the Americans might have resorted to such overkill. One explanation is that at the outset of the war, Washington did not see Iraq as a pushover. The Ba'thists had just successfully concluded an eight-year war (the longest in modern history) between themselves and Iran, in pursuance of which they had mobilized some one million troops, much of which mobilization, as already stated, was intact.[44]

Schwartzkopf, since he was determined to engage Iraq on the ground, must have been concerned about this battle-hardened force, especially if there were a chance he would have to fight it inside Kuwait City.

A look at a map will show that practically all of Kuwait is city. An Iraqi force entrenched inside the capital would have had to have been dug out, in what surely would have proved a costly campaign. Under the circumstances, Schwartzkopf would have insisted on a three-to-one superiority over Iraq, and since achieving that was impossible, he had to seek compensation. The only way of doing this was to rely on expansive use of technology.

The weapons used were of such lethality as to be in a category all their own—call them Star Wars weapons—for example, global positioning satellites, nocturnal scopes that permitted night fighting (when the Iraqis were blinded), and cruise missiles (which effectively are robot bombs). Many of these had never been tested under actual battlefield conditions, which is to say the Americans could not have known how they would perform, much less been able to determine their lethality.

Nonetheless, once the weapons' efficacy was shown, was there any need to pile it on, as it were, making so many bombing runs, destroying so much infrastructure?

As noted earlier, the Iraqis were remarkable in respect to the punishment they withstood; they never seemed to have considered the possibility of surrender (except at the very end when they were subjected to the full force of the American assault). The Americans might have foreseen such determination: ultra-nationalist regimes generally do not surrender. But the Americans, as we intend to bring out later, were (and remain to this day!) remarkably ill informed about the nature of their enemy.

In any event, given the fact that Iraq was adjudged formidable (*under certain conditions*), the Americans perhaps cannot be faulted for being overly cautious, even though the results in civilian casualties and infrastructure destroyed were appalling.

Ought not atrocity reports have militated for abatement? As we said above, *there were no atrocity reports*; the press was muzzled. Thanks to the infamous (from a professional journalistic standpoint) pool arrangements, few adverse reports were sent home. At the same time, however, even such revelations as the bunker incident (referred to above) failed to dent the American public's support of the war. On February 18, 1991, a poll of Americans showed that eight out of ten Americans believed the shelter was a military target and blamed the Iraqi government for the deaths of the civilians.[45]

For an ethicist, such behavior ought to have posed a problem. It was not so long ago that Americans—and Europeans—were condemning the Nazis for the bombing of Guernica. (Indeed, Picasso's painting of Guernica has achieved the status of an icon of resistance to tyranny.) If bombing civilians was bad when the Nazis did it, why did the Europeans and Americans condone it when it was the U.S. Air Force that was complicit?

PR

Part of the explanation lies with the promotion, by the Americans, of the so-called smart bombs, originally done to play up America's precision-targeting, a way of involving Americans (and the world) in the "scientifics" of the war. It soon became apparent, however, that the bombs were useful for overcoming squeamishness of those who, on ethical grounds, objected to bombing cities.

Soon the Americans were claiming that *their* war in Iraq to be *the most humane* ever conducted (see Schwartzkopf's claim cited previously).

Pure hokum. The bombs were not as prevalent in their use as claimed. They were extremely expensive, and that curtailed the numbers available. Along with that, as accurate as they are—like anything else mechanical— they malfunction.[46]

And what should never be lost sight of is the psychological damage the bombs do. Landing in heavily populated areas, as they were, they would always kill a few innocents. Additionally, what must it be like to be standing next to a building that suddenly evanesces? With a horrendous clap of thunder, a shower of fire! Does one get over that easily? (No nightmares?)

Be that as it may, Americans (as with anyone, anywhere) are prone to rationalize that which is unpalatable; they only want an excuse, and, if the smart bombs provided that, that was to the good—for the Americans.

Also effective in winning Americans over to the concept of air war was the argument that it spared *American* lives. If American ground forces did not have to engage, or if the engagement could be postponed while the enemy was softened up with bombing, this meant fewer body bags.

Fewer body bags. How many times did one who was associated with this war hear that phrase? Politicians were constantly wanting to know how many body bags there would be, with the threat implied that any number was too many.

At any event all of these objections came into play early in the war, and all one way or another were parried, a triumph of salesmanship, a theme we will revert to when we take up the activity of the neo-cons in Afghanistan and the second Iraq War.

One more point before we depart this topic. American propaganda also made the case that only war-related infrastucture was being hit. Even in cases where this was demonstrably not true, the Americans insisted that it was, and so it was presented in the media.

Here we have the law of unintended consequences operating at full spate. If electrical grids are targeted, it is with the intent of degrading the enemy's command-and-control; should the bombing succeed, the commanders are satisfied. But the bombing may also cause water purification plants to shut down, which causes diseases to spread. The appalling incidence of childhood mortality in Iraq, which came after the war, was mainly attributable to the malfunctioning of the country's water purification systems.

In other words, we are saying that, for a variety of reasons, America did not confront the moral implications of what it was doing. What was made to appear a plus—the fact the war was over swiftly—was that only from America's standpoint. To end it in a hurry, Washington perpetrated horrendous acts, against civilians mainly. There was no acknowledgment of this (at least the author is not aware of any such).

In any event, had America's harsh treatment of the Iraqis ended there, with the end of the war, perhaps one could say that the whole thing, while unfortunate, was not malign. However, the fact is that the brutality carried on into the postwar sanctions period, and it is that which we want to look at now.

Dual Containment

America's Dual Containment policy, initiated to keep up pressure on Iraq when the war ended, was the brainchild of Martin Indyk, a former director of AIPAC, and consequently a partisan of Israel.[47] Clinton made Indyk assistant secretary of state for Near East Affairs, which enabled him to shape America's foreign policy on a range of issues, including Iraq and the Gulf. The fact of that Clinton gave him such an influential post indicated that the president was abandoning evenhandedness in favor of all-out support for the Jewish state (essentially, what was happening).

The real danger of the appointment—as regards the Gulf—was it broke down the compartmentalization that formerly had obtained. When the oilmen were in charge (and for a while after) the Gulf was kept out of the Arab-Israeli dispute. Now, by bringing in a partisan of Israel and assigning him responsibility over Gulf affairs, Clinton was mixing the affairs of the two regions, which previous administrations had been at pains to keep separate.

The interesting thing is how Indyk was able to achieve this; that is, mix up the Israelis in the direction of affairs in this formerly buffered area. Effectively he made Dual Containment into an extension of

America's erstwhile Cold War policy, apparent from the choice of names—Dual *Containment*.

With the collapse of the Soviet Union, the great threat to the Gulf (which allegedly the Russians had posed) was no more. Further, Iraq had been defeated in the first Gulf War, and even before that—in the Iran-Iraq War—Baghdad had succeeded in laying low the Iranians.

So, effectively, *there was no threat to the Gulf* any longer and consequently no reason for the Americans to keep up a military presence there. Not so! said Indyk. The northern Gulf States, Iraq and Iran, remain a threat, to guard against which the presence was a must.

Setting to one side the untenability of this contention, Indyk's brain-child was ingenious. It gave the United States all that it could wish as far as the Gulf was concerned. It made provision for America's staying in the region militarily, *and that presence would be paid for by the sheikhs*. Hence, the policy of buying American protection, initiated many years back under the shah, would be maintained, in perpetuity, presumably.

However, it was in the area of oil matters that the new policy shone forth, so to speak. The original sanctions regime had an "oil-for-food" component. Although the United Nations surely never intended it to be so, the arrangement opened the way for the United States to take control of the international oil system. This is the same system that had functioned until 1973, when the major oil companies were expropriated by the producers. After that debacle, the concept of regulation ceased to have meaning. There appeared to be no need for regulating oil in a world in which consuming nations could not get enough.

Then, in a downturn in the world economy between 1981 and 1985, the Saudis put a floor under the price by playing the swing producer. In 1986, however, they abandoned that role, which caused chaos as prices sank to below $10 a barrel.

We saw how the first George Bush was able to work out an arrangement with Saudi King Fahd, whereby the Saudis and Americans would collude on keeping prices within a tight range of $14 to $17 a barrel. That arrangement somewhat obligated America to the Saudis, however. The Indyk approach of sanctioning Iraq and Iran returned the initiative to the United States. Effectively, the program became the mechanism whereby the United States could ensure an international oil price low enough to accommodate the United States but high enough to provide the revenue needs of the Saudis. That in turn would enable them to pay for the U.S. military to defend them.[48]

And how did it do this? By denying both Iraq and Iran the ability to sell their oil (except on extremely restrictive terms), Dual Containment created a shortfall in production that only one country could fill, namely Saudi Arabia. It was not generally recognized during the early days of the sanctions, but the big beneficiary was Saudi Arabia, which absorbed the quotas of both Iraq and Iran.

It was probably for this reason that the Saudis went along with the scheme originally; it seemed an advantage to them in a way that they found needful. But they ought not to have been so quick to embrace the shift.

By putting America's Gulf policy on a Cold War basis, Indyk laid the groundwork for the Pentagon to take over direction of affairs, and the Pentagon was where the Israelis' partisans in the United States—the neo-cons—were most entrenched.

The Best Laid Plans

In the early days of the sanctions, everything seemed to go swimmingly. The Ba'thists were recalcitrant, to be sure, but the Americans had confidence that, in time, one of two things would happened—either the Iraqis would rise in revolt against Saddam, or the latter would throw in the towel and seek some sort of face-saving solution for himself.

Not only did neither of these eventualities develop, it became apparent that the Ba'thists were consolidating their hold on the country. At that, the United States and its ally, Britain, decided to tighten the screws. They began taking more and more exception to what the Iraqis could legitimately import. Soon the sanctions authority was so curtailed that the Iraqis' life was hell. Things they had every right to possess were denied them on the basis that the items had dual-use aspects; that is to say, commodities that were meant to be used commercially, the Americans claimed, had a military application and so were withheld.[49] The strategy was to impress the Iraqis with the intolerableness of carrying on with Saddam, which would induce them to rise and drive him out.

It never happened. The uncooperative Iraqis refused to perform, and instead something quite untoward developed. Word began circulating of how deplorable conditions were inside the country. When several United

Nations, and non-governmental organization (NGO) officials spoke out against the harshness of the sanctions,[50] officials in Washington were forced to respond. Secretary of State Madeleine Albright's rejoinder was a classic of injudiciousness. She said the deaths of half a million Iraqi children ascribed to the sanctions was a price the United States thought worth paying to get rid of Saddam.[51]

To begin with, this was an awful thing to have said, but that aside, who had claimed that Saddam Hussein was a candidate for removal? America's Coalition partners (with the exception of Britain) had never signed on to such a thing. This was the first public indication of a changed American policy toward Iraq, and it also was the first move of the Americans toward unilateralism; that is, the propensity to go it alone, no matter what had been agreed to by the world body.

At this point, positions began hardening. Russia and France, and to an extent China, began demanding closure. They wanted the sanctions over with for humanitarian reasons, but also because some (if not all) of these states looked to resume trading relations with the Iraqis.

America dealt with this importuning by declaring a no-fly zone in the south of Iraq, supposedly to protect the Iraqi Shias. There was already a no-fly zone in the north of the country to protect the Kurds. The Americans then overflew the two regions, drawing the Iraqis' fire, which gave them—and the British, also participating in the overflights—opportunities of engaging the Iraqi anti-aircraft batteries on the ground.[52]

The daily exchanges enabled the Americans to claim that they were repelling Iraqi aggression, *when in fact what they were doing was creating the effect of a threat by behaving as if there were one.*

In other words, the strategy of the spectacle.

For a while, the Saudis and Kuwaitis (who along with the Shias and Kurds were supposedly being protected by this) went along. They kept up a pretense of believing that the flights and occasional bombing runs were necessary.

Ultimately, however, they began to grow restive. Among the Arab populations, the spectacle of Iraqis being tormented was galling. But along with that, the sheikhs were becoming alarmed by the behavior of the U.S. Defense Department. Under Clinton, Secretary of Defense William Cohen would make yearly trips to the area to sign the sheikhs up for more weapons buys. The sign-up sessions seemed, to the sheikhs, supererogatory; they were being asked to subscribe to many more purchases than were warranted given the nature of the threat (which, in this author's view, at this time was minimal).

Clinton and the U.S. Defense Department were treating the sheikhs as if they were milk cows, or at least this is the impression the sheikhs were getting. The fact of the matter was that they were not so affluent as the Americans supposed.

The Oil Factor

From the point of view of the Gulf States, the first Gulf War had been a disaster. The war had cost in excess of $114 billion, and the sheikhs (most notably the Saudis and Kuwaitis) had absorbed a good chunk of that expense. Not much was made of this at the time of the war (so much triumphalism was being expressed).

The difficulty began to be apparent in 1992, when the Saudis indicated they were having cash flow problems, and they might be forced to defer (or even renege on) weapons purchases from the United States. The amount in question was $14.3 billion.[53] Because of the way that the law in the United States is constituted, countries purchasing arms from the Americans have to set up a trust fund into which they pay—at regular quarterly intervals—a specified sum to cover losses were they to default.[54] The Saudis claimed they did not have the money and wanted Washington to waive payment (at least for a time). However, this was not possible. The Congress, which oversees such transactions, would not go along.

The situation seemed for a time to be stalemated.

Meanwhile, news that the Saudis were experiencing financial difficulty spread throughout Washington, causing consternation, particularly at the Pentagon.[55]

At the time, the Gulf States were spending more on American arms than was the Pentagon to equip its own forces. Without exaggeration, one could say that the Gulf was a mainstay (if not *the* mainstay) of the military/industrial complex, a situation that the United States had come to rely on—now more than ever, with the Soviet Union gone.

Adding to the Pentagon's discomfort, during this same time many of its overseas non-Arab customers were canceling orders because, in the aftermath of the Gulf War, the world had gone into a recession.[56]

Such setbacks were only to be expected, but through it all the Americans had believed the Gulf States would stay the course, and now even they (or at least the Saudis) were, in a manner of speaking, punking out.[57]

The initial response of many in Washington was to claim the Saudis were shamming. It was argued that, with Kuwait not producing any oil (after having had its fields sabotaged), and with the Iraqis not producing because of the sanctions (and the Iranians, too, having been embargoed), the Saudis ought to have been rolling in cash since they were absorbing the quotas of all three.[58] It was then brought out that the Saudis had been running deficits over the last ten years (deficits that they had contrived to keep secret). This had started in the 1980s with the worldwide recession and consequent rundown of the oil price. The Saudis had never climbed out of that hole. They had gotten by because the bankers, knowing they had the world's largest reserves of oil, figured they were good for the money—eventually.[59] But then the Gulf War hit and financially the Saudis were overwhelmed.

The Clinton Approach

The response of the Clinton administration to the Saudis' discomfort was to insist they fulfill their obligations. It is not known whether the Americans actually brought pressure, but some form of coercion must have been tried because the Saudis (it then became apparent) were reduced to disputing charges, something totally out of character for them.[60] They claimed that Prince Bandar, the Saudi ambassador in Washington, had committed the kingdom to purchases without getting government authorization.

In the end, it was agreed the five major contractors owed (McDonnell-Douglas, Hughes Aircraft, General Dynamics, FMC, and Raytheon) would stretch out their payments.[61] At the same time, under the deal the firms would collect their money in a novel way: they would form partnerships and borrow the amount from international lenders, with the Saudis guaranteeing repayment with interest.

The crisis looked to have been surmounted, but it then developed that Clinton expected the Saudis to make good on a further commitment to buy commercial airliners from Boeing and McDonnell-Douglas.[62] Clinton had a scheme of how the Saudis could manage this. He proposed the Ex-Im Bank guarantee the purchases.[63]

The Saudis ultimately went along with this arrangement as well, but not with what could be termed good grace. Indeed, even after the deal was publicized, no movement occurred on that front for an embarrassingly long time. The Saudis kept silent; either they were miffed or unsure how they were going to manage things.

Eventually, reality intruded on the Saudis' affairs. In 1999, they announced they would to have to cut defense spending. They would lop between $7 billion and $9 billion dollars by 2001.[64]

One–Two Punch

This move, which ought to have been anticipated, seems to have hit the Clintonites hard. They probably felt betrayed because, after all, they had contrived through Dual Containment to deliver the quotas of Iraq and Iran to the Saudis' hands. True, but along with that, they had saddled them with all those additional expenses, such as making them buy the commercial airliners, the Saudis did not want and could not afford.

What made the Saudis' desertion (as the Clintonites viewed it) so bad was that simultaneously they had "betrayed" the Americans in another area, that of oil.

In December of 1997, the Asia Meltdown occurred. The year before, the Saudis—in pursuance of their policy of accommodating the Americans by keeping up their oil production—had produced no less than $8.5 million barrels, an exceptionally high figure.[65] Thus, when the Meltdown struck and the Asians, in effect, pulled in their horns because their economies were contracting, the world experienced a severe oil glut.

The Saudis (certainly without their ever having meant to) had virtually single-handedly wrecked OPEC, as now all of their OPEC partners were experiencing profound financial difficulties. For a time, the members followed a beggar-thy-neighbor policy (the usual OPEC-response when difficulty strikes). Some went farther, however. Venezuela, which at the time had a right-leaning government, invited Western oil interests to buy into its then-nationalized fields, a move that Kuwait was quick to copy.[66]

However, when the Saudis indicated that they too would pursue such a scheme, Saddam Hussein lashed out violently, accusing them of throwing away the oil weapon.[67] The Saudis precipitously backed off their offer, but then the situation turned around, as unexpectedly the Populist Hugo Chavez took power in Venezuela, and his first move on assuming the presidency was to scuttle the offer for Westerners to buy into Venezuela's oil industry.[68]

Shortly after that, Venezuela, Saudi Arabia, and Mexico (a non-OPEC producer) announced that they would cut production to drive prices back up. Saudi Arabia cut from 8.5 million to 7.5 million barrels.[69] The price went from $14 a barrel to $27 a barrel in a matter of months.[70]

This was a hike that the Americans could barely accommodate. Indeed, it was the prelude to the popping of the Information Technology (IT) bubble, and the turnaround in the famous long-run bull market.

The Americans now had lost out all around. They no longer were coordinating oil policy with sheikhs, in particular with the Saudis, something they had been doing (and had gotten used to) since the first George Bush had gone to the Gulf in 1986.

This was particularly unwelcome thanks to a related development. America's domestic energy picture, which had been rosy (or at least the Americans perceived it so), had turned somewhat bleak. American oil companies were now spending more looking for oil overseas than at home, and most of their production and reserves were outside the United States. Indeed, America now ranked eleventh in terms of proven oil reserves and had slipped entirely from the list of top oil producers.[71] According to the American Petroleum Institute, an industry group, American production was in the midst of a "precipitous" decline.[72]

This was having an effect on the economy. Having to pay for overseas oil had added to the deficit, which had soared in 1996.[73]

One might have assumed that this was enough bad news. However, in addition to everything else, the sheikhs unexpectedly withdrew basing rights from the United States, and in some cases, went so far as to deny America overflight permission.

How did that happen?

Like much else that goes on in the world, it seems to have been triggered by a combination of things. First was the breakdown in security inside the kingdom. As we described previously, in 1995 a bomb went off in Riyadh, killing five Americans, one a U.S. Army sergeant. Then in 1996, Khobar Towers was blown up, killing seventeen U.S. military personnel.

We said earlier that, over U.S. objections, the Saudis concluded these were inside jobs, so to speak. Native Saudis had been growing restive because the Americans, after having assured them that they would leave the kingdom once the first Gulf War had ended, failed to do so.

To be sure, staying on was part of the agreement under Dual Containment, but the Saudi leaders could hardly tell that to their people. For the mass of Saudis, a continued presence of infidels in close proximity to the Holy Places was an abomination.

So once the acts of sabotage started, the royal family informed the Americans they would have to depart. The Americans did not refuse; rather they temporized, making a big show of withdrawing deeper into the desert—out of sight, out of mind.[74]

This did not work. What initially was mere discomfort on the natives' part soon ripened into rage; then the sabotage started.

It is significant that the Saudi leadership never actually demanded the Americans quit. The decision was rather forced on Washington, by none other than Saddam Hussein. In 1997, he provoked a confrontation with the United Nations by refusing to permit further weapons inspections. Saddam claimed that Iraq had given up all its weapons on the proscribed list, and, as a consequence, the intrusions were being unnecessarily prolonged. He also claimed the United States was using the inspections regime to keep Iraq in bondage.

Saddam did something else that was shrewd: he mounted a propaganda campaign aimed at his fellow Arabs, in which he made the point that, whereas Israel had admitted to having A-bombs (reportedly two hundred of them), no one was insisting *they* submit to inspections. Further (he said) Israel was occupying its neighbor, Lebanon—the United Nations was allowing that illegal occupation to continue.

The tactic of appealing to the double-standard proved efficacious, as the Arab governments were just then mired in negotiations with Israel over Palestine, negotiations that were going nowhere (about which we will have more to say in a moment).[75]

When the United States told Iraq that it must either reverse itself on the inspections issue or prepare for war, war seemed inevitable. But then, one by one, America's Arab allies deserted it. The sheikhs, as we said, withdrew basing rights and overflight privileges. Even Egypt and non-Arab Turkey refused Washington permission to use their territory as staging areas for the contemplated attack.

What these moves on the part of the Arabs and Turks signified was that America's position in the Gulf had now been effectively undermined.

The Americans had only just, with the Reagan administration, come to look on the area as vital to them. Now, with Clinton, they were being faced with the demand that they leave.

The Clinton Years

Before we end this chapter, we want to reprise the policy of the Clinton administration toward the Saudis. We feel that, under Clinton, America turned away from the House of Saud, in particular, and from concern about the Gulf States, in general; and this cooling of relations showed up in a number of areas. For example, when Bush left the White House, the United States was taking 46 percent of its oil from overseas, the bulk of that from the Gulf (of which Saudi Arabia was the largest contributor).[76]

Under Clinton, America moved to getting the bulk of its oil from Venezuela, Mexico, and Canada. By 1997, the Gulf States (which included Saudi Arabia) were selling only 19 percent of their production to the Americans.[77]

Given the fact that the ratio of Saudi oil imported to the United States reflected the state of relations between the two countries, it would seem that with Clinton, America underwent a policy change.

Another area where Clinton reversed the warming initiated by Bush was human rights. Under Clinton, the U.S. media returned to the practice of featuring human rights abuses in the kingdom. Much was made of the undemocratic nature of the Saudi government.

Another area where stress developed was over the Arab-Israeli dispute. Bush (the reader is perhaps aware) forced the Israelis under Yitzhak Shamir to take part in the Madrid talks with the Arabs, which launched the peace process. But then under Clinton, pressure on Israel, which had been kept up by Bush, was allowed to lapse, so that eventually it appeared to the world at large that the process was dead. When it was revealed in October 1993 that Israel and the Palestinians had been meeting secretly in Oslo, Norway, where they had, in effect, restarted the peace process, no one was more surprised than Clinton.

For a time, American-Saudi relations seemed to get back on track, as the Americans promoted a kind of Marshall Plan for the Middle East. In return for the Arabs and Jews making peace, America would sponsor a program to pump needed dollars into the economies of both countries.

However, when a right-wing fanatic assassinated Rabin, and Benjamin Netanyahu came to power, the Israelis reverted to shunning peacemaking with the Palestinians. The Americans pretty much accepted that.

When Barak replaced Netanyahu, peace was on the agenda once again. Clinton convened the Camp David talks and these, as mentioned in chapter 1, were seen by the Arabs as a sell-out by the United States of the Palestinian cause.

So, one could say that Clinton got what he might have expected when Saudi-United States relations turned sour.

But overall, the most extraordinary aspect of what went on was the ignorance the Americans displayed not just toward the Saudis but also toward the entire Arab world. Nothing better illustrates this than Clinton's handling of America's subsequent involvement with al Qaeda. When the really serious acts of sabotage started occurring, with the embassy bombings, the Americans discovered al Qaeda. However, as had occurred with Khobar Towers, they insisted on making a connection between this Arab group and Tehran. This, as we said in chapter 1, was simply untenable.

Al Qaeda is Wahhabi. The enmity between the austere Wahhabis and the Iranians (who are Shias) is (as we indicated in chapter 1) intense. Yet, the Clinton administration took the stand that Iran was sponsoring al Qaeda. It repeated this claim when the U.S.S. *Cole* was targeted.

It cannot be stressed enough: in the Middle East field, this was wrong-headedness to a degree that it is almost impossible to conceive. Unfortunately, there was worse to come.

Sanford Berger, Clinton's National Security Adviser, insisted America must retaliate for the embassy bombings, and he chose the target, a pharmaceutical factory in the Sudan. Berger claimed that it was in fact a chemical weapons factory owned by bin Laden. The Americans destroyed the factory with a cruise missile and later discovered that it was, indeed, a harmless pharmaceutical factory and not owned by bin Laden at all, but rather by a Sudanese businessman.

Where had the Americans gotten their information that this was a factory producing chemicals? Not from any of its own agencies—not the CIA or FBI. The intelligence came from "foreign sources." That could be only one of two countries—Israel or Egypt, both of which are ill disposed toward the Sudanese.[78]

To bomb an asset of a foreign country, in the foreigner's capital, based on intelligence derived from liaison is extraordinarily irresponsible. As might have been expected, when the truth was revealed about the nature of the factory, hostility toward the United States among Arabs soared.

Bin Laden was able to capitalize on this incident to underscore his oft-repeated claim that the Americans were waging a crusade against Arabs.

In any event, there is no question that, by the time Clinton left office, relations between the United States and the Arabs (Saudi Arabia in particular) had sunk to perhaps a lower level than 1967.

CHAPTER 5

The Neo-Cons' Silver Bullet Strategy

In this the last chapter we are going to try to explain what it was that caused the administration of George W. Bush to lead America into a quagmire, which effectively is what Iraq now constitutes.

The Bush team operated from a core of arrogance, believing the course on which it was embarked (in the name of the United States) had to succeed. The team members showed by their actions, and by their comments on events, that they believed what they were doing represented an advance for the whole of civilization, a move that, because it was progressive, could not be gainsaid. In other words, elements of the leadership sought to endow their performance with a moral justification.

In fact, what they were subscribing to was the principle of might makes right. They do not seem anywhere to have owned up to this, but that is what they were advocating. They acted on the assumption that, in the sphere of international relations, arms superiority was a trump. America had the most advanced weaponry, and that entitled it to do whatever it wished.

This was an extraordinary notion. Until 1991, no one in the leadership of the United States seems to have entertained such an idea. It was the first Gulf War—with its astounding display of American military prowess—that convinced influential parties in the United States that the way was now open to indulge in thinking of this sort.

We look at who promoted the attitude change, and we examine why their ideas caught on so widely. Elements of the society that, under normal circumstances, would not have gone along, did so, apparently with relish.

We want to examine this phenomenon of the Americans being so accepting of the war. We think it indicates something in their psyches, a certain fearfulness. This will lead us to try and look behind the thinking of America's rulers to figure out what really was motivating their decision to go to war. After all, three wars in one part of the world—two with the same country—in less than a decade is a lot of activity.

We think it was not so much Iraq the United States feared (or terrorism emanating from the likes of Afghanistan), but a potentially much more profound threat-the loss of America's hegemonic status.

An Opportunity Missed

Until the close of the Clinton administration, there was still an opportunity for the United States to work out a modus vivendi with the Gulf States, one that would have ensured peaceful relations. Bush could have revisited the intelligence surrounding the attacks on Khobar Towers, the embassies, the U.S. *Cole* and, in a manner of speaking, done the right thing; he could have moved to withdraw the U.S. troops from the Arabian peninsula.

This opportunity never was taken advantage of. This explains why America was so open and exposed to the Twin Towers atrocity. The Bush administration had tasked the intelligence community to find a link between sabotage in the Gulf and Iraq. So specific a charge blocked the CIA and FBI from investigating other areas.

Indeed, assuming that the CIA and FBI did find evidence of plotting by the al Qaeda group, they would likely have suppressed it. Why? Because the Bush administration *did not want* to hear that native Saudis wanted the United States out of the Gulf, and that they were so exorcised over this that they were resorting to acts of sabotage against American installations in the area. The whole aim of trying to establish a link with Iraq was to find an excuse for staying on there militarily.

So, this brings us back to the question we posed in chapter 1: why could not the Americans absorb the message that the Saudis were beaming at them with such intensity—get out! Get out! *Get out now!*

We will try to answer that one.

The Complex Exposed

The Persian Gulf was the rock on which America's military/industrial complex was grounded. The twin threats of Iraq and Iran were the best justifications the complex had for going on receiving subsidies from the American taxpayer.[1]

With the economy turning down, the Congress was in no mood to bankroll the Pentagon, an institution that now could be said to have become supererogatory. In effect, America was entering into an anti-defense-spending phase, similar to what overtook it in Vietnam days.

Were the twin threats from Iraq and Iran to disappear, not just the arms manufacturers would lose out. Most of the Pentagon's mignons—the Beltway bandits, the apparatchiks in the think tanks—these people, too, would suffer. Of course the Israelis and the Egyptians, who had effectively reinvented themselves to be America's first line of defense against terror, would have been devastated. Put bluntly, a whole culture was on the line.

In the early days of George W. Bush's administration, before 9/11, the major thrust of Pentagon activity was to seek economies. So great was the economizing that the period came to be known within the Beltway as the era of the Great Train Wreck.[2]

The situation of the military at the turn of the millennium did seem surely to be unraveling. At this point, literally out of the blue, relief appeared in the form of two airliners slamming in the Twin Towers in lower Manhattan.

What George W. Bush did as a result of Twin Towers was cut the Gordian knot. The policymakers in Washington had been wrestling with the problem of how to hang on in the Gulf (at no cost to the United States), and effectively they had gotten nowhere. Once the planes slammed into the Towers (and into the Pentagon in Washington), a solution materialized overnight, one that would get the Americans off the hook; however, U.S. leaders would have to be resolute if they meant to seize the opportunity.

We will never know, perhaps, but it does appear that something like the following was decided on. The Americans would declare war on Afghanistan and finish that country off as quickly as possible. Then they would move to settle with Iraq. They would overthrow the regime of Saddam Hussein—but more, *they would occupy the country*. Once Iraq was occupied, the problem of finding a base in the area would be resolved: *the base would be Iraq.* As for financing the Gulf force, that would be done on the backs of the Iraqis, using the revenue from the country's oil.

The solution was quite elegant, and there were even attractive add-ons. With an Iraqi puppet government set up, the Americans could hope to dominate OPEC, using the Iraqi delegation as their tool. They could also wield extraordinary influence over oil-starved countries such as Japan and Germany, who get the bulk of their supplies from the Gulf.

The problem was, how did one effectuate this scheme (assuming, that is, that our theory is correct)? How did one get from point A, the fact of America having a legitimate grievance against one country (Afghanistan, for having sheltered bin Laden, the alleged mastermind of the Twin Towers attacks), to point B (Iraq, which as far as anyone knew had nothing to do with the Twin Towers)?

The solution worked out by the Bush administration (and we assume it was primarily the neo-cons who were responsible for this) was to forge a connection in the public's mind between the unauthorized possession of weapons of mass destruction and terror. A terrorist was someone who either had such weapons, or aspired to get them. At one point in his career, Saddam Hussein had had them.[3] Osama bin Laden was a terrorist; therefore he would aspire to get them. Whence from? Iraq, of course. Why so? Because he and Saddam were both terrorists.

The logic was circular, but the pitch was slick. It effectively used Afghanistan—which America felt it had to go after because of what bin Laden, who was sheltering there, had done to it—as a springboard from which to dive into Iraq.

Of course, once devised, the strategy had to be implemented, and effectively this was carried out in two stages. The Bush administration first concentrated on selling the United Nations on the idea of America going to war. This it did by promoting the concept of "terror" as a great (indeed an *existential*) threat to all the world's peoples; terrorism had now became the new bogeyman, replacing communism.

To put its point across, the Bush administration sponsored conferences in the United States and Europe. Publicists barraged the media with horrific accounts of what lay in store were the terrorists not to be confronted. Bush personally lobbied the United Nations for a concerted international response to the looming threat. Once the United Nations agreed to go along, however, the Americans performed what basically was a bait and switch. They spurned offers of aid from their erstwhile

Coalition partners, announcing they would take care of this (that is, the operation of chastising the Afghanis) on their own. The effect was to marginalize the United Nations. By setting the United Nations on the shelf, which was what the Americans were doing, Washington could ensure against its meddling in the war.

Of course, there was a very real danger of the United Nations doing that, because the Afghan War was not, strictly speaking, legitimate. Afghanistan had not attacked the United States. Mullah Muhammad Omar, Afghanistan's president, made that point; he even went so far as to offer to turn over bin Laden to the Americans if Bush would supply him with evidence that the Saudi was truly involved in the attacks.

Bush rejected the proposal out of hand. The likelihood is that he did so because he did not have the evidence. To this day, Americans do not know what went on with those attacks, and there is every reason to believe that this is the case with their leaders as well.[4]

In any event, the war was on. Now what was needed was to sell it to the American public.

Ringing in the Christian Right

Here is where the neo-cons' strategy (again, always presuming it was they that got it up) proved effective. They cast the War on Terror in the guise of a "holy crusade." A crusade conjured up images of Christians fighting against Islam, thereby underscoring the fact of bin Laden and Saddam being Muslims. That the great Satan who threatened America's survival was *Arab* was an idea of enormous appeal to friends of Israel.

At the same time, making it out to be a crusade mobilized support from America's right-wing Christians. Since January 20, 1998, when Israel's then-premier (and leader of the Likud Party) Benjamin Netanyahu came to the United States to caucus with Jerry Falwell and Pat Robertson, right-wingers among the Jewish and American communities had been moving closer to an embrace.[5]

For their part, the Christians felt that a war such as the one the United States was contemplating fulfilled the prophecies. For them, the coming conflict was foretold in the Bible; it was part of God's plan.[6]

The right-wing Jews looked with favor on war against a Muslim state (*two* wars against *two* of them was almost too much of a good thing).

So, right from the first, Bush succeeded in enlisting support of two very powerful constituencies.

Still a war is a war. Americans do not like wars, and all Americans are not ideologically motivated, as were these two right-leaning constituencies.

Cost Efficiencies

What Americans mainly do not like about wars is their drain on finances. Their cost in lives of course is a factor, but that can be managed. More difficult is the financial aspect. Here the neo-cons were able to call on the air force for support. The airmen were claiming that wars of the future would be fought entirely from the air; ground troops would be obsolete.[7]

As noted previously, a sizable ground force had been assembled to fight the first Gulf War, but that was only at Schwartzkopf's insistence. The army engaged after thirty-one days of uninterrupted bombing of Iraq by air, bombing that so demoralized the Iraqis that, when the Americans finally did engage, the enemy capitulated immediately. The air force generals were promising now that this time around (in Afghanistan) there would be *no*, or practically no ground forces employed.

Wars are expensive precisely because of the necessity of using ground forces. The kind of wars the United States had fought until then required enormous long "tails." These actually are support trains. The trains are difficult to field and difficult to maintain in the field. As a consequence, it is usually the case that, when the trains are operational, expenses for war run high. Get rid of the army with its immense supply train (as the air force was proposing to do) and expenses would become minimal.

In this way, the neo-cons succeeded in co-opting the fiscal conservatives of the Republican Party, and that aspect of the affair probably proved crucial.[8]

A word of caution. Despite the apparent brilliance of the neo-cons' performance, it will not do to overestimate them. This was not a work of pure genius on their part. That is to say, we should not make the mistake of assuming we are dealing with a lot of super strategists who devised an approach that was irresistible, in and of itself.

The neo-cons' campaign did not succeed solely on the strength of its persuasiveness. The neo-cons had substantial support from within the

American elite establishment. The character of the neo-con movement had changed substantially since the Reagan years. Adherents of neo-conservatism could now be found at the very highest levels of government. Indeed, the mainstay of the neo-cons in Washington was a group called the Defense Policy Board. This outfit functioned as a kind of Committee of Imperial Defense, as had obtained under the British Empire.[9]

The individuals who sat on the board (appendix B) supplied the gravitas that undergirded the neo-cons' activities. There were also neo-con-generated support groups, such as the Project for a New American Century, which attempted to involve the United States in a war with Iraq during Clinton's tenure (appendix A).

This draws attention to a related fact: given that, under Clinton, the Democrats adhered to basically the same line as the neo-cons, the decision to fight cannot be laid at the door of one party. Rather, this was capitalism in action. The Open Door, Manifest Destiny, Reagan's crusade against the Evil Empire, and now, Bush's War on Terror, all should be seen as variants of the same strategy, the aim of which was to propel the ever outward expansion of the American empire.

And So to War, Once More

In Afghanistan, the air force took the lead, as planned. The focus of the campaign was to be on bombing, and the bombs (and missiles) were awesome. There was the newest generation of guided bombs, called joint direct attack munitions (JDAM), precision weapons guided by lasers that destroy targets as small as a single tank or a scud launcher, even when dropped from very high altitudes.[10] Apache helicopters came armed with sixteen Hellfire anti-tank missiles. Equipped with Longbow radar, the planes could fire at separate targets within seconds of each other.[11]

The infantry did participate, but mostly Special Operations units acting as spotters for the high-flying aircraft. The Special Ops personnel were equipped with hand-held transistors, which, when plugged into the global positioning satellite network, provided the targeting information necessary for the bombers to rain death on unsuspecting foes beneath.

It was enthusiastically claimed that America now had the armaments to accomplish in twenty-four hours what took seven days in 1991.[12]

As for those on the receiving end—the Taliban—it is a wonder how they stuck it so ferocious was the onslaught.

Effectively, there was nothing they could do. They either surrendered bin Laden and Omar, as Bush demanded, or made a stand of it. To be sure, the Americans had expected them to capitulate immediately, even before the war commenced. When that did not happen, the Pentagon clearly was surprised.

What the Bush administration ought to have realized was that the Taliban essentially was a tribal force, and tribesmen will always stand and fight because honor compels them to. However, once the tribesmen perceive that they are going to be defeated, they flee. No shame in it. It is pragmatic to the nth degree.

This is what happened. The Afghan War had but one set-piece battle, and that occurred outside Mazur e Sharif, on a strategic confluence of roads connecting the northern area of Afghanistan with the capital in Kabul.[13] The Taliban made their stand there in November, until the Americans called in B-52 bombers to carpet-bomb the area. After that, the Taliban fell back from the city, where they proceeded to melt into the countryside.

By December, it appeared that the Americans had no enemy left to confront. It had taken them only days to achieve this result, and if the war had truly ended here, this would have been a world's wonder—the United States lost but fifty-two men! It seemed that the air war proponents had proven themselves, stellarly.

Then came the cleanup—or perhaps we should say, the roundup phase. This, to put it charitably, was less successful.

Dissension in the Ranks

The Afghan opposition, which the Americans were counting on to ferret out the defeated Taliban, was not solidaric, at all. The bulk of the country is Pashtun, and these Pastun warriors, located in the south of Afghanistan, were mistrustful of (not to say at emnity with) the northern opposition, comprising Tajiks, Uzbeks, and Hazaras.[14]

The Taliban were also Pashtun, and thus, when it came to engaging the remnants of the Taliban fighters, the southerners were not to be relied on.[15] This meant the whole burden of the cleanup was going to have to fall on the Tajiks, the Uzbeks, and the Hazaras.[16]

But these latter were too shrewd to fall into that trap. Why take on the high-cost-in-lives operation of ferreting out the Taliban when every loss of theirs would unbalance the ratio of forces: Pashtun to northerners?

When the war was finally over, the Tajiks and the rest would want to be in as strong a position as possible so as to dispute with the southerners for rule over the country. The northerners wanted to avoid advantaging the Pastuns, who, under the Americans' original plan, would have been hugely benefited. Having sat out the war, they would have preserved their numerical superiority.

The Americans, who believed they had the defeated Taliban penned up in the mountainous Bora Bora area, urged the Tajiks, the Uzbeks, and the Hazaras to move expeditiously against them. The northern opposition leaders (actual warlords) demurred.[17] This left it to the Americans.[18] However, just one stab in that direction changed the Americans' minds after a team was ambushed and seven Americans died.[19]

The Americans then had recourse to bribery. CIA officers, packing suitcases stuffed with millions in low-denomination bills, went among the northern warlords, entreating them to take on the Taliban fighters.[20] Even this appears not to have succeeded, and so the Americans, in effect, simply called the whole thing off.[21] They walked away, leaving appreciable numbers of Taliban fighters holed up in the high mountain country along the Pakistan border (country that is so wild Pakistani police, who patrol the area, dare not venture there).

The Situation Today

Today it is impossible to tell who in Afghanistan is ex-Taliban, as those enemy fighters who did not flee to Pakistan simply have turned their coats. They have taken service with the victorious warlords, and since the Americans supplied the warlords with captured Taliban weapons, they even got their arms back![22]

What about the Afghanistan domestic scene?

On the ground, very little has changed.[23] Months after the war supposedly has ended (when this is being written) Afghanistan still is wracked by divisions; the warlords have taken over the country; the central government, under American sponsorship, is an anomaly, with a token Pashtun president surrounded by northerners who control all the important posts.[24] Recently, a constitution was voted, which supposedly will give more power to the president. It remains to be seen whether it will work. At present, the central government's writ does not run outside the capital (Kharzai, the president, cannot impose his choice of governor in most provinces, which are warlord-dominated).

Nor has the social life of the country improved. Afghan peasants have gone back to growing opium, even though the Americans had sworn to stamp this out.[25] Oft-predicted progress in democratizing Afghanistan has not materialized, and the condition of women seems to have reverted to what it was under the Taliban.

Finally, the refugees who fled at the start of the war have returned to a terrible bleak existence.[26] The NGOs, which are supposed to provide relief, are too overwhelmed to cope. Money to facilitate operations has gone missing. Countries that were forthcoming with donations at a donors' conference, have not delivered; the fund has practically dried up.[27] The United States made one large contribution when the war ended, and then waited months before making another, which has not been delivered as of this writing. American forces are not present in the countryside; they are only in Kabul, where they have pledged to guarantee Kharzai's safety.

Thus, it does not seem unfair to say that Afghanistan is back pretty much where it was in the period of the Russians' takeover. It is a scene of anarchy.

Most interestingly, neither Osama bin Laden nor Mullah Muhammad Omar has yet been apprehended.

Despite this, Bush was willing to break off his fight against terrorism to concentrate on Iraq, even as the Taliban was already reinfiltrating the occupied areas to resume their jihad.[28]

On to Iraq

Once again, the neo-cons took the lead with an ambitious campaign of propaganda, and in the process of doing so, exploited facts shamelessly. Facts were presented so as to be completely twisted. The neo-cons claimed, for example, that the Iraqis were part of a terrorist "axis of evil" and that they had weapons of mass destruction and means of delivering them—not only against America's Middle Eastern allies but also against the United States itself! All of which was quite ridiculous. The Israelis had destroyed Iraq's nuclear facility (Osiraq) in 1981, after which it had never been repaired. Even if the Iraqis had been able, covertly, to return it online, to produce a bomb, the notion they could have launched it against the United States was bizarre.[29]

America's erstwhile allies (except Britain and Israel) dug their heels in over this. They were not prepared to go to war with Iraq; they did not believe the charges about weapons of mass destruction; they did not believe in the alleged links between the Ba'thists and al Qaeda.

However, when the allies sought to counter neo-con claims with their own contradictory intelligence, the neo-cons, in effect, bullied them into submission. Even when influential voices within the U.S. defense establishment objected, the neo-cons repudiated them. General Eric Shinseki, the Army Chief of Staff, warned that it would take several hundred thousand American troops to occupy Iraq. Paul Wolfowitz, with no military experience, told him he did not know what he was talking about.[30] Anyway, according to neo-con Richard Perle, there would be no occupation, at least none that lasted over three months, because the Iraqi people were going to greet the Americans as liberators.

Where did Perle get such opinions? Largely from Ahmed Chalabi, head of the so-called Iraqi National Congress (a neo-con group), and a longtime exile from Iraq. Few inside the Beltway believed Chalabi. Indeed, he had been blacklisted by General Zinni when Zinni was CENTCOM commander; Colin Powell, too, refused to have dealings with Chalabi, a known liar.[31]

In fact, the whole neo-con campaign (the British as well as the Americans) seems to have been founded on lies. In the British case, there was the notorious "dodgy dossier," the claim about the Iraqis seeking yellow cake uranium in Niger and Blair's assertion that the Iraqis could deploy weapons of mass destruction in forty-five minutes.[32] On the American side, were the claims about mobile chemical laboratories, aluminum tubes for atomic bomb production, and meetings between Iraqi intelligence agents and al Qaeda operatives.[33]

Of course none of these lies could ever have gained credence had not the press cooperated. Objectivity, the hallmark of the profession, was trampled on. Journalists were satisfied to quote influential parties under attribution. Few took the trouble to follow up on the quotes to see if they made sense. Could they be substantiated?

Opposition, when it developed against the neo-cons' propaganda, came not from the press but from within the intelligence community. Analysts who had worked the Iraq accounts came forward to decry the neo-cons' fabrications. Such critics were overwhelmed, however, by (among others) outfits like Fox News, which seems to have regarded it as a duty to support the troops—even before the troops were committed or even before war was declared.[34]

A substantial peace movement developed in the lead-up to the second Iraq War, but this operated via the Internet, that is, outside the orbit of the established press. For a time, demonstrations against the war were large. Bush ignored them. After one particularly large and angry one, the president was asked if this would have any affect on his policymaking. He said, "You know, size of protest, it's like deciding, well, I'm going to decide policy based on a focus group."

In effect, one could say the second Iraq War—as had been the case with the first Iraq War and Afghanistan—was a done deal. The thing would go off no matter what because powerful interests expected it to.

Psychic Rewards, and Some Material Ones

Many parties have benefited already from the war. The friends of Israel certainly have. With Iraq destroyed, there is one less Arab power about which the Israelis have to be concerned. The arms merchants have a veritable new lease on life.[35] Companies that had been retrenching because contracts were not materializing, now are running in the black.[36] Before the Afghan War, money for the Pentagon was tight; now the military can count on getting whatever it needs (or maybe, we should say, wants). In a time of economic uncertainty, some $379 billion was appropriated for defense by a willing Congress, unconcerned as to from where the money would come.[37] Defense-related firms, such as Halliburton and Bechtel, have done marvelously from the war, snagging lucrative contracts worth billions, without competitive building.[38]

The oil companies, interestingly, seem to be holding back. The biggest companies—Exxon-Mobil, BP-Amoco, Royal Dutch/Shell and Chevron-Texaco—are refusing to enter Iraq until the security situation has improved. However, no one should doubt that when things do settle down, the majors will move in—or return is perhaps a better way of putting it.

Then we have the apparatchiks—people like Wolfowitz and Perle, the professional war-promoters. They are assured a good living for at least the foreseeable future.[39]

Finally, we have the right-wing Christians. They have not benefited materially as much as psychicly. Bush has enhanced their status, giving them all sorts of rewards, such as vitiating Roe v. Wade; passing the Patriot Act; giving bigots like General Boykin a platform from which to express his hateful sentiments (without official reprimand, interestingly).[40]

The Great Fear

This brings us to the matter of change to American society because of the war. Here we will be indulging in some speculation, which seems legitimate—so close to events, it is hard not to speculate.

America has, since the time of Reagan, been moving rightward, a drift that seems to accelerate with each passing year. The whole neo-con phenomenon, one could say, is a manifestation of this rightward-moving tendency.

As to what has occasioned it, we have to seek an explanation in psychology. Let us revert to our discussions in chapter 3 about growth. Americans seem to have come to the realization that unlimited growth—thought to have been inevitable prior to the 1960s—is no longer so. This awareness (we believe) developed as far back as the late 1950s, with the nuclear freeze movement and the hysteria over radiation, manifest in the strontium 90 scare. Until then, atomic energy had been thought a great panacea, something that would preserve America's edge as a world leader, but that (more importantly) would permit standards of living to go on rising, despite the increase in the world's population, which threatened the "haves."

When atomic energy, instead of inspiring confidence occasioned fear, Americans recoiled. Immediately they were subjected to a further traumatizing revelation that grew out of the OPEC Revolution. Energy, which Americans believed was theirs to control through the major oil companies, was taken from them and given to the producers—the greatest wealth transfer in history! As Americans viewed the matter, *all of that wealth was going to Arabs.* It is from this juncture that we date the stereotypical caricature of Arabs, so prevalent in the United States, as venal, grasping sheikhs.[41]

Americans are human; that is to say they are fallible. Faced with a great disappointment, they seek a scapegoat. The Arabs have become the villains who can be blamed for what Americans perceive as a great injustice done to them (the taking away of so much oil wealth).

Things did not improve after the 1970s. Going into the 1980s, under Reagan, America appeared to regain confidence (Reagan was nothing if not a great confidence-inspirer). But then the Great Communicator stumbled. Not only did supply-side economics not restart growth (Reagan's own vice president ridiculed it as "voodoo economics"); Reagan himself— the man—was seen to be vulnerable over Iran-Contra.

By the late 1980s, America was retrenching on a number of fronts. Japan and Germany, conversely, were on the rise. Talk was of a new power balance—a multi-power one. The economic leaders, Japan and Germany, would demand to share power with the Americans.[42] If one studies Wolfowitz's now-famous 1992 Strategic Guidance Directive, one can see that it is aimed primarily at the Germans and Japanese.[43] Wolfowitz is there laying out a strategy whereby the United States will not have to share with anyone; he is telling Americans they can rely on the their armed might.[44]

Science may have failed in one area, but not to worry! The United States was still the most technologically advanced in the weapons field. Whatever Americans wanted they could *seize*. Of course, what Wolfowitz was suggesting implied abandoning collective security. But then, collective security—the neo-cons would have us believe—functions to restrain the vigorous, the strong societies, like that of the United States.

We believe this essentially is what has been going on with Iraq. America has invaded because, since 1986, Washington has come to see that, if it is to preserve its status as world hegemon, it must control oil, and to control oil it must regulate the production of OPEC. In our view, all of the wars that America has been fighting—the first and second Iraq Wars and the one in Afghanistan—have been over resources.[45] This being the case, the real contest on the world's stage today is that of the industrialized northern countries against the poor, resource-rich, but nonetheless deprived southern ones. The United States, were it to be allowed to continue making its way unchallenged, would surely seek to impose northern (or, more specifically, Anglo-Saxon) control over resources, which are in an ever-tightening supply.

We want now to offer our prognosis of where the Americans are headed.

The Prognosis

We said earlier that what Americans chiefly dislike about wars is their expense. This is what made the neo-cons' strategy so appealing. They held out a prospect of fighting wars on the cheap. The United States would exploit its superior weapons technology to cow its enemies. Implied was that the United States might not have to fight at all—it would be sufficient to threaten an enemy with destruction to have him back down.[46]

As we say, that was the scheme.

We have no intention of going into detail over the conduct of the second Iraq War. One thing, however, has come out strongly—the thing has not worked out as the neo-cons planned. The Iraqis have succeeded in hurting the Americans. This has not been a casualty-free war for the United States. (As of this writing, America's toll has passed 700.) By forcing the Americans to fight in the cities, the Iraqis have leveled the field somewhat. Combat in the cities is more one-on-one. It cuts down on America's advantage, which, viewed dispassionately, is the ability to stand off and kill from a distance. In the cities, American soldiers, no matter how well equipped, are vulnerable, as is being proved daily in Baghdad, Faluja, and Najaf.

So, it would appear that the neo-cons' strategy has been compromised. What is the effect of that likely to be? It is very difficult to say. To be sure, the aura of unassailability, which formerly enveloped the neo-cons, has now been dissipated. When Bush asked the Congress to appropriate an additional $87 billion to fund the occupation, it certainly shocked the fiscal conservatives. The neo-cons had not led them to believe that anything like that would go on.

Further, it has come as something of a shock to Americans that their erstwhile Coalition allies will not help them out in this crisis. There really ought not to be surprise over this. Having been excluded from the decisionmaking that led up to the war, the Allies feel themselves to have been *dissed*, as we say.

Then, on top of that, there is the matter of closure. The neo-cons' strategy depended on the war being over quickly. Only in that way could

Bush avoid a backlash from Americans who had been called to serve in Iraq. Now the troops there have had their tours extended, which was bad enough for the regulars, for many reservists it has proved a disaster. This, in turn, seems to have provoked a falling off in enlistments for the reserves.

And finally, what about the oil that was going to finance this whole operation? The Iraqi resistance has been dogged in its determination to sabotage the facilities, and over and above that, it appears, because of the dreadful harsh sanctions, that Iraq's facilities have been degraded. The Iraqi oil industry cannot be made to turn a profit for years.

We have one more point to make before we wrap it up and give our conclusion.

Expressing the Unexpressable

To make an argument for the Ba'th and for Saddam Hussein today is practically unthinkable, but that only shows the power of the propagandizing that has gone on about Iraq.

In fact, in their contest with the United States, the Ba'thists did have a moral position—nothing less than self-determination. After all, what was it that was being fought over?

Answer: how Iraq was to dispose of its oil.

Essentially, then, the fight of Saddam with the Americans differs not a great deal from that of Mosadeq with the British. Both men felt they had a right to exploit their national treasure to suit the needs of their country. Consequently, both defied the will of those who were managing the oil system at the time, and both paid for their boldness.

The difference between the Iranian and Iraqi was that enough time had passed for the Iraqi to benefit from hindsight. Mosadeq had tried to go it alone. Saddam recognized he needed a system, one that comprised his fellow OPEC members. Saddam was experienced enough to appreciate that the hold the industrialized northern states had over Iraq was their ability to deny it, and all of the other high absorbers, the right to set its own production levels. He also appreciated the game the Kuwaitis and UAE sheikhs were playing, how they, by cheating on their quotas, helped the Americans. Saddam gave evidence that he understood when, during his interview with April Glaspie, he specifically accused the sheikhs and the Americans of waging "economic war" against him.

When Saddam made his announcement about enforcing OPEC dis-cipline on the sheikhs, he almost certainly was reacting to pressure he felt was being put on him. It is unlikely he was thinking in terms of leading a fight of the producers against the consuming states. He was not, in other words, setting himself up to be a champion of the resource-rich but poor southern tier countries.

Nonetheless, once he made his stand that was the role he assumed, of leading a fight against the Americans (and by extension the Europeans) over who was to control oil. Saddam's decision constituted an explicit challenge to the Bush-Fahd arrangement whereby Saudi Arabia and the United States had earlier agreed to collude on oil production, and thus mutually control OPEC.

This is what more than anything—we feel—sealed Saddam's fate. If anyone doubts it, look at what happened to Venezuela's Hugo Chavez when he made a similar move to buck the system. Did the United States not try to overthrow him in a coup, one strikingly reminiscent of that which was successfully brought against Mosadeq?[47]

With a strong Iraq in the enforcer's role, OPEC could have become something it never was—a legitimate cartel, one that would work for the producers.

As we say, such ideas are not fashionable today and probably will become less so as the charade of bringing the Ba'thists to trial is affected. Still, unless the neo-cons can succeed in completely distorting the record, these matters eventually will have to be set to rights, at least we certainly hope so.

Conclusion

Over the years, America allowed itself to be drawn into a lucrative arms-trading relationship with the monarchs of the Persian Gulf. The relationship was an attractive one, in as much as it returned lots of petro-dollars to the United States, or more specifically to the military/industrial complex. But it had an added economic effect. Through contracts with the monarchs, America was able to influence their oil policies.

So, one could say that there was double pay-off here. The Americans got needed cash through arms sales, and, along with that, they got what amounted to a usufruct over oil production (worldwide). That, of course, influenced the world economy, which, in turn, enhanced America's status in its role as hegemon.

The year 1988–1989 appeared as a historic conjuncture, where three trends came together that imperiled America's position in the Gulf. The Soviet Union collapsed; that removed the reason for America staying on in the region, militarily. Iraq defeated Iran in the Iran-Iraq War; that removed the threat of a militant Islamic Republic. And, finally, the so-called high absorber states in OPEC appeared set to turn that institution into a bona fide cartel, which would have served their interests against those of the United States.

This last was most threatening to the Americans because to affect the changeover of OPEC to an instrument of the high absorbers would have reduced the sheikhs (America's allies) to negligible quantities. They would have had no influence in OPEC, and hence their collusive relationship with the Americans would have been brought to an end, thus also ending America's usufruct over oil.

To balk this radical realignment, which the high absorbers were essaying to bring about, America sought to pressure Iraq, which it viewed as the architect of the scheme, and this backfired into provoking a war. At the end of the war, anti-Iraq elements in the Clinton administration proposed that, rather than disengaging its forces from the region, the United States stay on to keep an eye on Iraq and Iran, so they could not recover.

The Clinton administration claimed that Iraq and Iran constituted a threat to the sheikhs. It proposed that the sheikhs allow the United States to resume protecting them; the sheikhs would, in effect, become enablers because they would finance the protection by continuing to buy arms from the military/industrial complex. Had this arrangement been effectuated, it would have returned the Gulf to the status quo ante of Cold War days.

What Washington failed to perceive was the contradiction that an American military presence in Saudi Arabia would pose. Given the religious sensibilities of the natives, America could not expect to preserve their erstwhile goodwill, as long as it was—in the Saudis' eyes—profaning their sacred shrines. Indeed, the decision to stay on infuriated some elements of Saudi society, and instances of sabotage against the Americans began to proliferate.

Rather than seeking to resolve this situation peacefully, the Bush administration (egged on by the neo-cons) tried to force the issue by exploiting the horrific attacks on Twin Towers and the Pentagon.

Effectively, today, the whole of the Gulf (not to mention the wider Muslim world) is enflamed against America. If Washington means to defy this opposition, it will have to lay out large sums of cash, since it seems likely that America's base in Iraq, to which it transferred from Saudi Arabia, will be under continual siege.

However, if our assessment of the neo-cons is correct, this fact (of the military presence proving costly) will not be allowed to become a deterrent to staying on. In fact, the neo-cons will welcome the activity of the Iraqi resistance, because continued violence against American troops will make necessary continued subsidization at higher and higher levels of the military/industrial complex, and will practically ensure underfunding of social programs in the United States, which is what the conservatives have been agitating for since the end of World War II; that is, to dismantle the New Deal.

Which brings us to our conclusion: the stance that the neo-cons are adopting is untenable. It is going to lead to increasing friction at home in the United States, as Americans' standards of living are depreciated by having to pay more and more taxes to support the military, and it will bring about a corresponding deterioration of America's position internationally, as states on the periphery are prevented from exploiting their resources, which will be channeled to the center, namely to the United States and its allies.

In other words, what the United States has lost by this imperialist power grab of Iraq—and by extension of the Gulf—is its moral authority, which, we think, counts for something. Of course the neo-cons have their own morality. History will judge.

Appendix A
Letter to President Clinton on Iraq

January 26, 1998

The Honorable William J. Clinton
President of the United States
Washington, DC

Dear Mr. President:

We are writing you because we are convinced that current American policy toward Iraq is not succeeding, and that we may soon face a threat in the Middle East more serious than any we have known since the end of the Cold War. In your upcoming State of the Union Address, you have an opportunity to chart a clear and determined course for meeting this threat. We urge you to seize that opportunity, and to enunciate a new strategy that would secure the interests of the U.S. and our friends and allies around the world. That strategy should aim, above all, at the removal of Saddam Hussein's regime from power. We stand ready to offer our full support in this difficult but necessary endeavor.

Project for the New American Century. Available online at http://www.newamerican century.org/iraqclintonletter.htm

The policy of "containment" of Saddam Hussein has been steadily eroding over the past several months. As recent events have demonstrated, we can no longer depend on our partners in the Gulf War coalition to continue to uphold the sanctions or to punish Saddam when he blocks or evades UN inspections. Our ability to ensure that Saddam Hussein is not producing weapons of mass destruction, therefore, has substantially diminished. Even if full inspections were eventually to resume, which now seems highly unlikely, experience has shown that it is difficult if not impossible to monitor Iraq's chemical and biological weapons production. The lengthy period during which the inspectors will have been unable to enter many Iraqi facilities has made it even less likely that they will be able to uncover all of Saddam's secrets. As a result, in the not-too-distant future we will be unable to determine with any reasonable level of confidence whether Iraq does or does not possess such weapons.

Such uncertainty will, by itself, have a seriously destabilizing effect on the entire Middle East. It hardly needs to be added that if Saddam does acquire the capability to deliver weapons of mass destruction, as he is almost certain to do if we continue along the present course, the safety of American troops in the region, of our friends and allies like Israel and the moderate Arab states, and a significant portion of the world's supply of oil will all be put at hazard. As you have rightly declared, Mr. President, the security of the world in the first part of the 21st century will be determined largely by how we handle this threat.

Given the magnitude of the threat, the current policy, which depends for its success upon the steadfastness of our coalition partners and upon the cooperation of Saddam Hussein, is dangerously inadequate. The only acceptable strategy is one that eliminates the possibility that Iraq will be able to use or threaten to use weapons of mass destruction. In the near term, this means a willingness to undertake military action as diplomacy is clearly failing. In the long term, it means removing Saddam Hussein and his regime from power. That now needs to become the aim of American foreign policy.

We urge you to articulate this aim, and to turn your Administration's attention to implementing a strategy for removing Saddam's regime from power. This will require a full complement of diplomatic, political and military efforts. Although we are fully aware of the dangers and difficulties in implementing this policy, we believe the dangers of failing to do so are far greater. We believe the U.S. has the authority under existing UN resolutions to take the necessary steps, including military steps, to protect our vital interests in the Gulf. In any case, American policy cannot continue to be crippled by a misguided insistence on unanimity in the UN Security Council.

We urge you to act decisively. If you act now to end the threat of weapons of mass destruction against the U.S. or its allies, you will be acting in the most fundamental national security interests of the country. If we accept a course of weakness and drift, we put our interests and our future at risk.

Elliott Abrams
Richard L. Armitage
William J. Bennett
Jeffrey Bergner
John Bolton
Paula Dobriansky
Francis Fukuyama
Robert Kagan
Zalmay Khalilzad
William Kristol
Richard Perle
Peter W. Rodman
Donald Rumsfeld
William Schneider, Jr.
Vin Weber
Paul Wolfowitz
R. James Woolsey
Robert B. Zoellick

Appendix B
Members Policy
Review Board

Kenneth Adelman, former aide to Defense Secretary Donald Rumsfeld

Richard Allen, former National Security Advisor

Martin Anderson, policy advisor for the presidential campaigns of Ronald Reagan, Pete Wilson, Bob Dole and George W. Bush (Center for Public Integrity, 3/28/03; Hoover Institution Newsletter, 2001)

Gary Becker, Nobel Laureate in Economics

Barry Blechman, founder and president of DFI International, a consulting firm

Harold Brown, former Secretary of Defense under Carter

Eliot Cohen, professor and director of the Strategic Studies Program at Johns Hopkins University, Paul N. Nitze School of Advanced International Studies

Devon Cross, Executive Director of the Donor's Forum

Gen. (Ret.) Ronald R. Folgelman, Air Force

Thomas Foley, former Speaker of the House of Representatives

Tillie Fowler, former Congressional Representative

Newt Gingrich, former Speaker of the House

Gerald Hillman, Managing Director of Hillman Corp.

Gen. (Ret.) Charles Horner, Air Force

Fred C. Ikle, former Undersecretary of Defense for Policy

Adm. (Ret.) David Jeremiah

Henry Kissinger, former Secretary of State under Nixon

Adm. (Ret.) William Owens

Dan Quayle, former Vice President

Henry Rowen, former Assistant Secretary of Defense for International
Security Affairs

James Schlesinger, former Secretary of Defense

Gen. (Ret.) Jack Sheehan, U.S. Marine Corp.

Kiron Skinner, professor Carnegie Mellon University

Walter Slocombe, attorney for Washington D.C. office of Caplin &
Drysdale

Hal Sonnenfeldt, director of the Atlantic Council of the United States

Ruth Wedgwood, professor of law at Johns Hopkins University

Chris Williams, former Special Assistant for Policy Matters to Defense
Secretary Donald Rumsfeld

Pete Wilson, former California Governor

James Woolsey, former director of CIA

Notes

Chapter 1

1. See "Election Jars Algeria's Rulers," *Washington Post*, December 30, 1991; "Jordan Keeps a Wary Eye on the Islamic Surge in Algeria," *Financial Times*, January 29, 1992; and "Algeria's New Muslims," *Washington Post*, January 27, 1992.

2. In the West, much was made of this concession of the king, and when the Muslim Brotherhood (see below) gained five portfolios in the government, winning twenty-two of eighty seats in the parliament, this was construed as an ominous development. But it was no such thing. The Brotherhood was always (and continues to this day) to be one of the firmest props to the throne in Jordan.

3. "Tunis Chief Calls for Arab Repression of Militants," *New York Times*, January 5, 1992.

4. For background on Sunni-Copt antagonism, see John Waterbury, *The Egypt of Nasser and Sadat: The Political Economy of Two Regimes* (Princeton, N.J.: Princeton University Press, 1983), 360–3. The specific incident referred to occurred in the summer of 1991 in the Cairo neighborhood of Imbaba (more on Imbaba later).

5. "War and Politics Clog Azerbaijan's Road to Riches," *New York Times*, July 2, 1993; "Afghan Fighters Aiding Azerbaijan in Civil War," *Washington Post*, November 8, 1993.

6. The author heard these stories repeatedly when he toured the Maghreb and Jordan-Israel in 1992.

7. For the reason that popular unrest in the Middle East (as perhaps is the case elsewhere) once unleashed is difficult to control and likely to turn on the possessing classes, which the wealthy sheikhs constituted.

8. The fall occurred in 1986 and was triggered by a price war between the Saudis and non-OPEC producers, primarily Britain. For details see chapter three, also the author's *Iraq and the International Oil System—Why America Went to War in the Persian Gulf* (Westport, Conn.: Praeger, 2001).

9. It is estimated that foreign debts of at least $34 billion were eating up 75 percent of Algeria's hard currency earnings.

10. *Balad* simply means "country," in the sense of "neighborhood," or "down-home," or "homeboy"—the roughly equivalent meaning in the United States.

11. The IMF maintains that it did not enter into a formal relationship with the Algerians until after the riots occurred; hence any reforms undertaken were not at its behest. A number of sources dispute this. See "Islamic Plan for Algeria is on Display," *New York Times,* January 7, 1992.

12. The authorities, as would be expected, put the toll much lower.

13. The author was told this on his trip to Magreb and Levant in 1992.

14. This was an important victory, since, in Algeria, the mayors are dispensers of patronage.

15. The author, while in Algeria just after the trouble, was shown film footage taken by intelligence operatives of the interplay between the speakers and those in the crowd who were haranguing them. There are precedents for this kind of activity in the West, the so-called red priests, but it is in the East, particularly in Constantinople under the Orthodox confession, that the phenomenon was most encountered. See Steven Runciman, *The Great Church in Captivity* (Cambridge: The University Press, 1968), 53.

16. *Mujahadeen* simply means one who strives for the faith.

17. The author is aware that in Egypt, the craze of rich young Egyptians to acquire Gucci bags and designer jeans obviously puts the very poor at a disadvantage. For many of these, it was a relief to drop out of the competition by adopting the austere style of dress of the pious.

18. When the author first went to Egypt in 1969, when Nasser was still in power, young Egyptians attending class at the American University in Cairo would frequently arrive at the school wearing the *imalaya laf* (the head-to-toe body covering) only to step inside the school grounds, doff the wrap, and emerge looking like any trendy European youth. When Sadat took over, the same youth openly flaunted their European dress in public, and it was coincidentally that the trend for more modest garb began to burgeon.

19. Algeria's revolution was called the Revolt of the Million Martyrs and was largely fought by urban and rural guerrillas; it lasted eight years.

20. This was Mustafa Buya Ali, who was shot to death in the midst of one such attempt.

21. One of the first histories in English of the Brotherhood (by an American scholar), which is still useful, is Richard Mitchell, *The Society of the Muslim Brothers* (Oxford: Oxford University Press, 1969). The Brotherhood started before World War II and was originally committed to restoring the Caliphate, which had disappeared after World War I. The Brotherhood also calls for reinstitution of *shari'a* (religious) law.

22. The author has been regaled with accounts of the hardships undergone by the Brothers during research expeditions to Egypt.

23. Sadat was himself a longtime member of the Brotherhood, one of the few Brothers among the Free Officers.

24. See Robert Springborg, *Mubarak's Egypt* (Boulder, Colo.: Westview Press, 1992).

25. Ibid.

26. To this day, the author is not convinced of this theory. Nonetheless, evidence in favor of it is persuasive. Sadat supposedly boasted just before his death of how he humiliated the Supreme Guide of the Brotherhood (whom he had arrested), making him crawl before him literally. Something like that would certainly have enflamed passions against him.

27. The author was in Cairo during the riots and, in fact, was caught up in them, thus having a good opportunity to observe them firsthand.

28. The author witnessed, for example, the crowd overturn Mercedes-Benz cars and set them afire, and shatter the windows of shops selling Western appliances.

29. Sunnis, of course, are the major orthodox sect of Islam.

30. Practically a whole literature exists on this fellow, who lived for a time in the United States and was implicated in the assassination of Jewish activist Meir Kahane (more about him later).

31. For discussions of the police–villager relationship, see *FBIS-NES-92-126*, June 30, 1992, "Sinful, Bloody Battle Viewed." For reports on attacks on police and the escalating nature of these attacks, see *FBIS-NES 91-155*, November 25, 1991, "Islamic Groups, Security Forces Clash," and *FBIS-NES-90-1033*, May 29, 1990, "Police Vehicle Attacked, Four Officers Injured."

32. "Egyptian Leader Calls for Patience after Quake Victims Riot," *New York Times*, October 18, 1992.

33. This was the story given to the author by the head of Egypt's security.

34. See "Visitor Attacks in Egypt Spread to Cairo," *New York Times*, February 14, 1993, sec. v, p. 3, and "2 Killed and 16 Hurt in Blast in Central Cairo Coffee Shop," *New York Times*, October 27, 1993.

35. Mubarak, like Sadat before him, was a military man. The ruler of Tunisia, Muhammad Ali, was an ex-security officer. Only in Morocco was there no military. Israel's ruling elite is primarily comprised of officers.

36. The coercion was partly the work of the United States, which refused to accept them into the United States. Thus, they were practically forced to go to Israel.

37. On the causes of the revolt, see Aryeh Shaley, *The Intifadah: Causes and Effects* (Jerusalem: The Jaffe Center for Strategic Studies, 1991).

38. See Ze'ev Schiff and Ehud Ya'ari, *The Intifadah: The Palestinian Uprising— Israel's Third Front* (New York: Simon & Schuster, 1989).

39. See Ziad Abu-Amr, *Islamic Fundamentalism in the West Bank and Gaza* (Bloomington: Indiana University Press, 1994).

40. Whereas the PLO had a reputation for being overly bureaucratized and corrupt.

41. Another religious group, Jihad (which we will discuss later), called for the use of firearms against the Israelis at this point; arms, until then, had been banned by the Palestinian leadership. "More on Islamic Jihad Decision to Use Firearms," *Amman Al Ray*, November 26, 1990, *FBIS-NES-90-208*, October 26, 1990.

42. See "New Leadership in the Territories Analyzed," *Ha'aretz*, February 12, 1989, *FBIS-NES-89-030*, February 15, 1989.

43. At the peak of the intifadah (the end of 1990), 9,972 residents of the territories were being held in military detention facilities. Of this number, 4,401 had already stood trial, 1,332 awaited trial, 3,477 were being held until proceedings were ended, and 762 were administrative detainees. Approximately 4,000 others were being held in the prison service installations, of which 1,7173 were being held until legal proceedings were completed. At this time, there were four main detention centers. They were the installation on the beach at Gaza, which held some 1,025 Palestinians; Zahiriyah Prison, holding 493 prisoners; two large detention centers inside Israel, one holding 5,915 Palestinians and another 1,532. Statistics are taken from "Betzelem Report Sums Up Three Years of Intifadah," *Ha'aretz*, December 5, 1990, *FBIS-NES-90-239*, December 12, 1990.

44. These often have adolescent-type names such as the Red Eagles, the Black Panthers, and so on.

45. After this was written, an incident developed in Spain, which illustrated neatly the point we are making here. A journalist for *Al Jazeera*, the Qatar television station, was arrested and accused of funneling funds to al Qaeda (more about this later) in Afghanistan. The journalist replied that he was merely transferring zakat money to religious charities in the Kabul, and that the money was collected in Spain from among the Arab exile community

most of whom were Muslim Brothers. "Spanish Judge Harbors Bias, Says Reporter In Terror Case," *New York Times*, December 14, 2003.

46. For background on the CIA's role in organizing the mujahadeen, see John Cooley's *Unholy Wars* (London: Pluto Press, 1999). It is also likely that the agency, in recruiting for the mujahadeen, worked through the charitable organizations that collected the zakat. Also that Osama bin Laden (about whom more later), in running the operation for the CIA, made use of the *hawla* network, whereby the charitable groups passed money collected from the sheikhs around the world.

47. The Saudi government always claimed a population figure higher than it had, but among Middle East hands this was simply discounted. Suddenly, in the 1990s, it became apparent the figure had actually shot up.

48. It is not unusual that this would be the result, given the depressed employment situation all over the Third World at this time.

49. Assad perpetrated the atrocity at Hama in 1982, where, it has been estimated, some 5,000 Brothers were massacred.

50. In 1992, the army sent the author to investigate the Islamic Fundamentalism phenomenon, an investigation that involved touring the Magreb, the Occupied Territories, and Jordan.

51. "Mosque Raid Stirs Criticism of Police," *New York Times*, March 12, 1993.

52. "Mubarak Cautions Islamic Extremists," *Washington Post*, March 5, 1993.

53. "Israel Seeking to Convince U.S. that West is Threatened by Iran," *Washington Post*, March 5, 1993. Israel did not have to worry about Islamic Fundamentalists; it did however have a concern about America (under Clinton) renewing calls for progress on the peace process. Bush had pressured Rabin's predecessor, Yitzhak Shamir, into attending the Madrid Conference.

54. It is interesting to compare the coverage of the media on Fundamentalism before and after the Middle Eastern rulers' visit. An initial spate of stories, which appeared in 1991 and early 1992, addressed the problem in general terms. "U.S. Aide Calls Muslim Militants Big Concern in the World," *New York Times*, January 1, 1992; "Tunisia Faces Renewed Threat from Islamic Fundamentalists," *Washington Post,* January 11, 1992; "Moslem Militants Polarize Arab World," *Financial Times*, January 14, 1992; "The Saudis are Fearful Too, As Islam's Militant Tide Rises," *New York Times*, December 31, 1991; "A Fundamentalist Finds a Fulcrum in the Sudan," *New York Times*, January 29, 1992; "Tunis Chief Calls for Repression of Militants," *New York Times*, January 5, 1992; "Election Jars Algeria's Rulers," *Washington Post*, January 19, 1992; "Jordan Keeps a Wary Eye on Islamic Surge in Algeria," *Financial Times*, January 29, 1992; "Algeria's New Muslims," *Washington Post*, January 27, 1992. Coverage diminished considerably after

the curbing of the FIS in Algeria and then shot up again before the visits to the United States of Rabin and Mubarak. Now the emphasis was on a specifically Iranian fundamentalist threat. "Islamic Fundamentalist of Iran Rushing to Fill the Void Left by Evil Empire," *Philadelphia Enquirer*, January 5, 1993; "Muslim's Fury Falls on Egypt's Christians," *New York Times*, March 15, 1993; "The Snake of Terror in Our Garden," *Wall Street Journal*, March 5, 1993; "Fundamentalists Last Spasm of the 20th Century," *New York Times*, April 6, 1993; "Egypt, Algeria Assail Iran for Backing Rebels," *Washington Post*, April 8, 1993, and "A Terrorist Network in America?" *New York Times*, April 7, 1993. Typical of the content of these latter stories is this excerpt from a Charles Krauthammer piece in the *Chicago Sun-Times*, December 31, 1992, "Iran Grows as Threat to West": "As with the Soviet Union, the new messianic creed must be contained. This means aid—material and political—to those fighting to contain Iran and its emanations. It means, at the least, halting the reckless traffic with Iran in dual-use (civilian and military) high technology. The new threat is as evil as the old empire."

55. "Bomb Tapes Put Agents' Role at Issue," *Washington Post*, August 4, 1993.

56. Ibid.

57. Ibid.

58. "Mosque Raid Stirs Criticism of Police," *New York Times*, March 12, 1993.

59. Conversations with Saudi intelligence officers.

60. John K. Cooley, *Unholy Wars* (London: Pluto Press, 1999).

61. This tells what sort of organization al Qaeda really is: it is a network. Bin Laden has the lists of those who served in Afghanistan and can draw on them for individuals to undertake specific operations. But al Qaeda has no more organization than that, and so is not an existential threat to the United States.

62. We say "assume" because we do not know whether he was behind the attacks. The Americans have never revealed their evidence for saying it was he.

Chapter 2

1. We regard systems as attempts by groups and/or individuals to organize activities to control them. In the case of the international oil system, what was being organized was the oil industry, and it was done in a coercive manner; that is, a few of those companies that engaged early in producing and selling oil continued through various machinations not only to preserve their preeminent positions as industry leaders, but they eventually were able to sew up all of the significant production sources. For further

elaboration of this view, See my book, *Iraq and the International Oil System: Why America Went to War in the Persian Gulf* (Westport, Conn.: Praeger, 2001).

2. The mandates were put in place at the end of World War I, and supposedly were set up to ease the transition of territories within the old Ottoman Empire into the modern era by equipping them to become democracies. In fact, Britain and France used the mandates to exploit the wealth of the region over which they had charge. Since Iran (then called Persia) did not fight in the war, neither Britain nor France had any sway over it. However, British commercial and financial interests had been penetrating the country for some time, which brought Britain great influence there.

3. The French also had a smaller stake through the Compaigne Française des Petroles (CFP).

4. As the name suggests, Royal Dutch was originally a Dutch concern, and the Dutch retain considerable interest in the firm until this day. But before World I, the company was angling to take over the Shell Oil Company, a British outfit. During World War I, the company's chief executive, Henri Deterding, made approaches to the British government with the aim of securing British involvement (for involvement read protection) for his company. See the author's *Iraq and the International Oil System*, 30; also Robert Henriques, *Sir Robert Waley Cohen* (London: Seckler & Warburg, 1966), 414.

5. See E. H. Davenport and Sidney Cooke, *The Oil Trusts and Anglo-American Relations* (New York: Macmillan, 1924), 1–44.

6. For details on exchanges between British and Americans over this, see ibid.

7. Anthony Sampson, *The Seven Sisters* (New York: Viking Press, 1975), 75.

8. Britain also had an interest in Burmah Oil, but beyond that nothing.

9. The British set up an organization, the British Controlled Oil Fields Group, which ranged all over the globe looking for fields. For background on this see Pierre l'Espagnol de la Tramerye, *The World Struggle for Oil* (New York: Alfred Knopf, 1924), 11, 143, 166; Frank Hanighen, *The Secret War* (New York: The John Day Co., 1934), 152, 165; Anton Mohr, *The Oil War*, (New York: Harcourt Brace, 1926), 209, 213; L. Vernon Gibbs, *Oil and Peace* (Los Angeles: Parker, Stone & Baird, 1929), 40, 58, 70.

10. Sampson, *The Seven Sisters*, 79–80.

11. Davenport and Cooke, *The Oil Trusts and Anglo-American Relations*.

12. Specifically, the companies had to develop a British connection. This applied as well for the Gulf Corp. going into Kuwait and Standard Oil of California going into Bahrain. In the latter case, the Americans incorporated in Canada.

13. Daniel Yergin, *The Prize* (New York: Simon & Schuster, 1991).

14. Ibid.

15. This was Caluste Gulbenkian, so-called Mr. Five Percent. Gulbenkian, who put together the original deal that led to the formation of the IPC, controlled 5 percent of the company shares.

16. Mostafa Elm, Oil, *Power and Principle* (Syracuse, NY: Syracuse University Press, 1992), 31.

17. J. H. Bamberg, *The History of the British Petroleum Co.* (Cambridge: Cambridge University Press, 1994), vol. II, 37.

18. Elm, *Oil, Power and Principle*, 29–30.

19. Before Reza Pahlavi took power, the British dealt with the tribes, principally the Bakhtiaris, who provided protection for the fields. The British were not at all happy to see Reza crush the tribes and take over that role, as it meant they were limited in their ability to manipulate the government by playing off the tribes against it.

20. Peter Sluglett, *Britain in Iraq, 1914–1932* (London: Ithaca Press, 1976).

21. The best backgrounder on this episode is *The International Petroleum Cartel Staff Report to the Federal Trade Commission, Submitted to the Subcommittee on Monopoly of the Select Committee on Small Business*.

22. See Sampson, *The Seven Sisters*, 45.

23. Ibid.

24. For the background on this, see David Painter, *Private Power and Public Policy* (London: I. B. Tauris, 1986), 33.

25. Ibid.

26. John M. Blair, *Control of Oil* (New York: Pantheon, 1976), 39.

27. Ibid.

28. For background on this, see Irvine Anderson, ARAMCO, *the United States and Saudi Arabia* (Princeton, N.J.: Princeton University Press, 1981).

29. See J. H. Bamberg, *The History of the British Petroleum Co.*, vol. 11, 303.

30. Blair, *Control of Oil*, 39.

31. See Robert M. Collins, *More: The Politics of Economic Growth in Postwar America* (Oxford: Oxford University Press, 2000).

32. Europe previously had run on coal. But the war had killed many of the miners, and, along with that, many European politicians feared to see the resurgence of the powerful miners' unions. It made more sense economically to switch to oil.

33. The industry had been concentrating its production in the Gulf before and during World War II. In part, this was owing to a revival of nationalism in South America, particularly Venezuela, which the oilmen deplored. See

Pelletière, *Iraq and the International Oil System*, 136–37, for a discussion of the shifting center of gravity of the oil business.

34. See Anderson, *ARAMCO, the United States and Saudi Arabia*, 188, and Blair, *Control of Oil*, chap. 3.

35. There is an apparent contradiction here: what about the Red Line Agreement? Supposedly, under it the Cartel was able to restrict oil deals anywhere in the old Ottoman Empire, not just among its own members but by anyone. How could Standard of California move in then? The actuality was that Britain had no particular influence over the Saudis, because it had backed the clan of the Rashidis against the Saudis, and when the Rashidis lost out, so did the British.

36. Anthony Sampson, *The Seven Sisters*, 170f.

37. Ibid.

38. According to Painter, *Private Power and Public Policy*, 171, in 1950 ARAMCO paid the U.S. government $50 million in income tax and the Saudis $66 million in royalties. In 1951, claiming taxes paid to the kingdom, ARAMCO paid only $6 million in U.S. taxes and $110 million in royalties to the Saudis.

39. Bamberg, *The History of the British Petroleum Co.*, vol. II, 324–26.

40. The British and Soviets occupied Iran during World War II so they could ferry supplies via the Gulf to the Caspian Sea to the Soviets.

41. Mohammad Mosadeq, whom we will introduce shortly, actually started the agitation for the review of the concession before World War II, when he was a deputy in the *majlis* (parliament).

42. Bamberg, *History of the British Petroleum Co.*, vol. II, 401.

43. Mohammad Reza Pahlavi, in his autobiography *Mission for My Country* (New York: McGraw Hill, 1961), has a long, derisive account of Mosadeq's negative nationalism philosophy.

44. Mostofa Elm, *Oil, Power and Principle*, 267.

45. Bamberg, *History of the British Petroleum Co.*, vol. II, 401.

46. Painter, *Private Power and Public Policy*, 180.

47. The involvement was not acknowledged in the United States until the CIA agent who ran the coup, Kermit Roosevelt, published his memoirs, *Countercoup: The Struggle for the Control of Iran* (New York: McGraw Hill, 1979), wherein he revealed the details.

48. For how the Tudeh behaved, see Mazir Behrooz, *Rebels with a Cause* (London: I. B. Tauris, 1999).

49. The shah, in line with the traditional Iranian attitude toward balancing, believed Tehran at all costs must keep the favor of Washington, to wield against London.

50. Gary Sick, *All Fall Down* (New York: Viking Penguin, 1986), 16.

51. Eisenhower believed that the national economy might be bankrupted if driven too hard, or its free enterprise character fatally compromised by a regimented Cold War mobilization. The trick, as Eisenhower saw it, was to figure out a preparedness program that would give America a respectable position without bankrupting the nation. Robert M. Collins, *More: The Politics of Economic Growth in Postwar America*, 55.

52. Bamberg, *The History of the British Petroleum Co.*, vol. II, 491.

53. "Every gun that is fired, every warship launched, in the final sense, is theft from those who hunger and are not fed, those who are cold and are not clothed. The world in arms is not spending money alone. It is spending the sweat of its laborers, the genius of its scientists, the hopes of its children," Dwight Eisenhower.

54. Ann Markusen and Joel Yudkin, *Dismantling the Cold War Economy* (New York: Basic Books, 1992), 39.

55. Ibid., 40.

56. Ibid.

57. Ibid., 41.

58. Ibid.

59. Ibid., 42.

60. Ibid., 43.

61. The concept of space exploration, issued in during the Kennedy years, obviously also added to the space industry. The payroll for the National Aeronautics and Space Administration (NASA) grew tenfold under the Apollo Program. By 1965, the agency and its private contractors employed 411,000. NASA appropriations rocketed from less than $1 billion in fiscal year 1961 to $5.2 billion in fiscal year 1964; Robert M. Collins, *More: The Politics of Economic Growth in Postwar America*, 54–55.

62. For a discussion of this aspect of the business, see Markusen and Yudkin, *Dismantling the Cold War Economy*, 44.

63. Ibid.

64. Qasim refused to allow the Communist Party recognition, instead he encouraged some Iraqi leftists to form a new Communist Party, which was loyal to him personally. For details see Uriel Dann, *Iraq Under Qassem* [sic] (London: Frederick A. Praeger, 1969).

65. Yergin, *The Prize*, 522.

66. Ibid.

67. The best account of Qasim's dealings with the oil companies is in David Hirst, *Oil and Public Opinion in the Middle East* (New York: Frederick A. Praeger, 1966).

68. Uriel Dann, *Iraq Under Qassem.*

69. In 1964, the author went as a journalist to interview Barzani in northern Iraq. This involved being smuggled over the Iraq-Iran border, an operation that was facilitated by the shah's security apparatus, SAVAK. It was common knowledge among journalists at the time that the shah was sponsoring the Barzani revolt, and his action in assisting not only the author but other newsmen to illegally enter Iraq to cover the Kurdish story would seem to prove it.

70. Interestingly, too, there is some evidence the Ba'th came to power through connivance with the CIA. See Hanna Batatu, *The Old Social Classes and the Revolutionary Movements in Iraq* (Princeton, N.J.: Princeton University Press, 1978), 985; Marion Farouk-Sluglett and Peter Sluglett, *Iraq, Since 1958* (London: I. B. Tauris, 1987), 83; and Edith Penrose and E. F. Penrose, *Iraq, International Relations and National Development* (London: Ernest Benn, 1978), 288.

71. Adil Hussein, *Iraq, The Eternal Fire,* (London: Third World Center for Research and Publishing, 1981).

72. For Israel's negotiations with the Iranians over oil, see Uri Bialer, *Oil and the Arab-Israeli Conflict, 1948–1963* (London: Macmillan, 1999).

73. On the shah's attitude toward Arab Nationalism, see his autobiography, *Mission for My Country*, chap. 13.

74. The American invasion of Lebanon was, by all accounts, a fiasco. There were no very effective communists in Lebanon, nor any great threat of any kind. The Lebanese met the Marines coming ashore on the beaches of Beirut selling them bottles of Coca Cola.

75. For a discussion of the anomalies and the primativeness of the early Ba'thsits, see my book *Iraq and the International Oil System.*

76. Given the difficult political climate in Iraq, it is no wonder the opinion persists that this was not an accident; apparently it was.

77. Aref claimed that the first lot of officers that moved against him were backed by the CIA. See Hannah Batatu, *The Old Social Classes and the Revolutionary Movements of Iraq* (Princeton, N.J.: Princeton University Press, 1978), 1066.

78. The exposure came through the leaking of the secret Congressional report on the affair to *The Village Voice*, February 23, 1976.

79. Markusen and Yudkin, *Dismantling the Cold War Economy*, 56.

80. Ibid., 79.

81. Ibid., 82.

82. Ibid.

83. John Lewis Gaddis, *Strategies of Containment* (Oxford: Oxford University Press, 1982), 320.

84. For the shah's career of arms buying see Anthony Sampson, *The Arms Bazaar* (New York: Viking, 1977), chap. 14.

85. The shah actually bought so many arms the top brass in the Pentagon became alarmed and counseled Nixon to rein him in because "he couldn't possibly use all the stuff he was buying." M. Reza Ghods, *Iran in the Twentieth Century* (Boulder, Colo.: Lynne Rienner, 1989), 261.

86. Jude Wanniski, *The Way the World Works* (Washington, D.C.: Regnery, 1878), 218f.; also, Collins, *More*, 68f.

87. Wanniski, *The Way the World Works*, 222.

88. Ibid., 220.

89. Robert M. Collins, *More*, 68.

90. When King Idriss let contracts for Libya's oil, he specifically excluded the majors, concentrating instead on small independent companies. When Gadhafi decided to break the Cartel, he focused on these small outfits, threatening to cut off their supply. Because these companies in most cases had no alternate sources of oil, they were forced to give way.

91. See Sampson, *The Seven Sisters*, 268f.

92. American law forbade the companies to behave as a cartel, which, of course, is what they were. If they wanted to negotiate collectively, they had to get the government's permission.

93. Ibid.

94. "The Oil Companies in the Crisis," in the *Oil Crisis in Perspective*, ed., Raymond Vernon (New York: W. W. Norton, 1976), 183.

95. In Jeffrey Robinson, *Yamani: The Inside Story* (New York: Atlantic Monthly Press, 1989), 80.

Chapter 3

1. An indication of this was the unwillingness of the Congress to appropriate funds for a Rapid Deployment Force in the area after the Soviet invasion of Afghanistan, the refusal of the Carter administration to take military action when the Islamic Republic seized American hostages, and Washington's refusal to interfere when the shah seized three small islands in the Gulf, which belonged to one of the UAE.

2. As it was during all the time the British and the oil companies held sway there.

3. Nixon deputized the shah of Iran to be America's surrogate in the Gulf in 1972, which effectively would mark the entry of the United States into the area.

4. The reader should note that only one year after the United States undertook to safeguard the stability of the area, it was supplying arms to the Kurds to destabilize the legitimate government of Iraq.

5. Iraq has only one port, Basrah, which can only be reached by sailing up the Shatt. By signing away half the Shatt to Iran, Saddam seriously limited Iraq's access to the Gulf.

6. Many of the shah's public utterances about this time were quite cutting about the West. See Yergin, *The Prize*, 638, and Sampson, *The Arms Bazaar*, 249. Treasury Secretary William Simon, at this time, commenting on some of the shah's more extreme statements, called him "a nut"; Yergin, *The Prize*, 644.

7. The shah had cancer at this time, which he kept concealed.

8. Yergin, *The Prize*, 637–38.

9. Under the Shia form of Islam, the mullahs are almost entirely dependent on donations to fund themselves and their works, and the principal contributors, traditionally, are the bazaaris.

10. Other than the near war with the Iraqis discussed above, the only other one the Iranians fought at this time was a small-scale affair in Oman.

11. For an excellent description of how this corrupt dealing was carried on, see Gerald Howson, *Arms for Spain* (New York: St. Martin's Press, 1998), 203f. Also for corruption over arms dealing in general among Iranians and Americans, see Anthony Sampson, *The Arms Bazaar*, 234.

12. Overall defense spending, measured in constant dollars, fell 32 percent between fiscal year 1969 and fiscal year 1975. Collins, *More*, 1–5.

13. Ibid., 66, 68.

14. Ibid., xi; also 22, 29.

15. Ibid., 202. The previous big buildup had come under Kennedy when the United States prepared to fight two and a half wars simultaneously. That cost the country $17 billion in additional defense appropriations. Collins, *More*, 56.

16. Ibid., 202.

17. One could argue that neo-cons' roots go back even further than the McGovern days; that they actually derive from the campaign for Soviet Jewry, identified with Senator Henry Jackson. This is where the leading neo-con, Richard Perle, first attracted notice.

18. Apropos of this, there is the information that the Ba'thists, a civilian group, deliberately kept a tight check on the military, which in Iran and Iraq formed the new class (or caste), which was largely responsible for the profligate lifestyle.

19. The reader should be aware that throughout all this time, the leader of Iraq was General Ahmed Baker, Saddam's mentor. The general was ailing, however, and it was Saddam who more and more came to run the government.

20. Saddam apparently had the Ba'th Party meeting at which the alleged conspirators were exposed videotaped and then circulated cassettes of the proceedings.

21. The majority of Iraqis are Shias, who have always mistrusted Pan-Arabism, because they believe that in any merger of Iraq with another Arab state the Shias would lose their numerical advantage as they are submerged in a larger pool of Sunnis. The Kurds, who are not Arabs, oppose for roughly similar reasons.

22. The party was always structured extremely hierarchically, a holdover from the days when it mainly functioned underground. Consequently, one could not move up in the party until one was thoroughly vetted, a time-consuming process.

23. Said Aburish, *Saddam Hussein and the Politics of Revenge* (New York: Bloomsbury, 2000), 124.

24. Ibid., 197.

25. The rebels who overthrew the Hashemites gunned down the royal family in the palace; the regent, Abdillah, and the prime minister, Nuri As Said, were literally torn apart by the mob.

26. For a discussion of Qasim's reforms, see Hanna Batatu, *The Old Social Classes and the Revolutionary Movements of Iraq* (Princeton, N.J.: Princeton University Press, 1978), 888.

27. Said Aburish, *Saddam Hussein: The Politics of Revenge*, 114.

28. The problem is that the United States, which was monitoring events in the north of Iraq throughout the Iran-Iraq War, never raised the alarm about this alleged atrocity. One has either to accept the Americans' defense that no such attacks took place (see the CIA's report on *Iraq's Weapons of Mass Destruction Programs*, October 4, 2003) or concede that this was a coverup— that the United States knew and deliberately suppressed the information.

29. As evidence of this interpretation, we would cite Saddam's nationalizing of Iraq's oil industry; no one who is looking forward to building up his Swiss bank account so he can go into comfortable retirement (à la South American dictators), takes on the oil industry.

30. To be sure, the Iraqis were advantaged in ways the Egyptians were not. For example, the demographics set them apart. Iraq, with a relatively small population (which the Ba'th expanded) was better off than Egypt weighed down with 70 million. But then the author is not aware that the Egyptian leadership ever seriously sought to tackle the population problem.

31. Aburish, *Saddam Hussein: The Politics of Revenge*, 114.

32. Ibid.

33. Phebe Marr, *The Modern History of Iraq* (Boulder, Colo.: Westview, 1985), 269.

34. Before the Iran-Iraq War, Iraq could be classified among Group II nations with an annual GNP over $3000 per capita. Peter Pellet, "Sanctions, Food, Nutrition and Health in Iraq," in *Iraq Under Seige*, ed. Anthony Arnove (Cambridge, Mass.: South End Press, 2000).

35. According to Aburish, Iraq's oil income went from a "pitiful" $572 in 1972 to $5.7 billion in 1974; *Saddam Hussein: The Politics of Revenge*, 106.

36. Ibid., 110.

37. Ibid.

38. Ibid., 109.

39. Ibid., 147.

40. Not only did the Saudis have the land space to accommodate an extensive U.S. presence but they also had been building infrastructure since 1974, which the Americans could use. Hence costs could be kept down.

41. Nicholas Laham, *Selling AWACS to Saudi Arabia* (Westport, Conn.: Praeger).

42. The special relationship between Washington and Riyadh became formalized in 1974 when Prince Fahd signed a military and economic cooperation agreement in Washington, and immediately after that Nixon visited Riyadh. Ian Skeet, *OPEC Twenty-Five Years of Prices and Politics* (Cambridge: Cambridge University Press, 1988), 120.

43. The Saudis moved up the spending curve slowly. In 1974, their tab was $2.6 billion. By 1985 it was up to $23 billion. Correspondingly, the Americans' share of weapons being supplied the Saudis also climbed. In the early 1970s it was 51 percent; by 1979 it was up to 79 percent. Abbas Alnasrawi, *Arab Nationalism, Oil and the Political Economy of Dependency* (Westport, Conn.: Greenwood, 1991), 114.

44. This was the situation in the United States where inflation did not start coming down until 1981, while the United States remained in the grip of a recession.

45. Yergin, *The Prize*, 755.

46. Sheikh Ahmed Zaki Yamani, "Oil Price Collapse Part of Western Plan to Dominate OPEC—Yamani," *OPEC Bulletin*, June 1986.

47. It could do this because the sharp rise in oil prices made it profitable to exploit the North Sea beds, which previously had been neglected because the process was too costly.

48. Yergin, *The Prize*, 748.

49. An outfit like OPEC is always at the mercy of so-called free riders, companies that seek to undercut the Cartel's price, just by a little bit, but enough to draw buyers away from the Cartel members. Obviously, OPEC cannot tolerate behavior like this and must move to squelch it.

50. It was called net backing, and essentially, under it, the Saudis would guarantee oil companies who contracted to buy their oil that, were the price to fall after the contract was signed, the Saudis would make up the money the companies would have lost.

51. Ibid.

52. Yergin, *The Prize*, 748.

53. Americans may have believed this late in the game (the mid-1980s) that they were self-sufficient in oil, but that was a delusion. According to testimony in Congress in 1977, America had been importing a greater and greater percentage of oil even before the OPEC Revolution. In 1975, 30 percent of America's oil came from OPEC, and it was expected that that figure would rise to 50 percent by 1985. The Subcommittee on Energy of the Joint Economic Committee the U.S. Congress, *Energy Independence or Interdependence: The Agenda with OPEC* (Washington, D.C.: Government Printing Service, January 13, 1977).

54. The problem was that members cheated, and unless there was someone to rein them in, prices could not be exploited most profitably.

55. "Bush to Seek Saudis' Assistance in Stabilizing Plunging Oil Prices," *New York Times*, April 2, 1986.

56. "Possibility of Oil Price War Spells Trouble in the Southwest," *New York Times*, December 17, 1985.

57. "Saudi-U.S. Deal Suspected on Oil Price," *Washington Post*, January 10, 1992; "U.S. Tries to Influence Oil Prices, Papers Show," *Washington Post*, July 21, 1992.

58. "The Rising Price of Oil," *Washington Post*, April 21, 1986.

59. *Christian Science Monitor*, July 31, 1987.

60. Aburish, *The Politics of Revenge*, 186.

61. Ibid., 188.

62. The main reason they did so was the mullahs looked on the military as the principal bearers of the ideology of modernization. But on a more basic level, the military constituted the arrivistes who had oppressed the poor.

63. Which led Western intelligence officers to conclude that the Iraqi army, while no good on the offensive, was formidable when fighting defensively on its own soil.

64. Dilip Hiro, *The Longest War* (New York: Routledge, 1991), 118.

65. The best source on this period is the author's book *The Iran-Iraq War: Chaos in a Vacuum* (Westport, Conn.: Praeger, 1992).

66. All of these details can be found in *The Tower Commission Report* (New York: Bantum Books, 1987).

67. Ibid.

68. "U.S. Official Suspects Israelis Sent Ethiopia Cluster Bombs," *New York Times*, (January 21, 1990; "Noreiga 'Advisor' Mike Harari Interviewed," *Foreign Broadcast Information Service*, January 6, 1990, TA060121590; "An Israeli in Panama: Whose Broker? *New York Times*, January 11, 1990; "Isareli Tied to Suspect Colonel is Discovered Slain in Miami," *New York Times*, January 24, 1990; "Two Columbians Arrested in Scheme to Buy Missiles," *Washington Post*, May 8, 1990; "Ethiopian Army Stops Rebel Advance," *Washington Post*, February 10, 1990; "Israeli Arms Ticketed to Antigua, Now in Columbian Drug Arsenal, *New York Times*, May 6, 1990; "United States Troops Seize Israeli Regarded as Top Noreiga Advisor," *New York Times*, December 28, 1989; "Israelis Aided China on Missiles," *Washington Post*, May 23, 1988; "Israeli Consultants Should be More Careful," *Washington Post Outlook*, September 3, 1989; "Israeli Hired Guns," *New York Times*, September 8, 1989.

69. "Global Arms Sales Rise Again, and the U.S. Leads the Pack," *New York Times*, August 17, 2001.

70. For details on this see Anthony Sampson, *The Arms Bazaar*; Ann Markusen and Joel Yudkin, *Dismantling the Cold War Economy*; Ken Silverstein, *Private Warriors* (New York: Verso, 2000); and Andrew Pierre, *Cascade of Arms: Managing Conventional Weapons Proliferation* (Washington, D.C.: The Brookings Institution, 1997).

71. For details, see *The Tower Commission Report*.

72. Conversations by the author with various officers who participated in these exchanges.

73. The reader has to be aware that the Ba'thists, since they fell back across their border in 1982, had been scrabbling to convince Iraq's public that they could survive and eventually overcome Iran. They were on the road to securing that confidence, when the Al Faw debacle hit them.

74. *The Tower Commission Report*.

75. Conversations with American officers stationed in Baghdad. This confrontation came at a Congress of the Ba'th held in Baghdad. *The Baghdad Observer*, July 14, 1986.

76. See the author's treatment of these battles in *The Iran-Iraq War: Chaos in a Vacuum*.

77. For a discussion of how the Iraqis were able to effectively reconfigure their forces to go over to the offense, and do it in secret, see my book *Iraq and the International Oil System*.

78. It was generally believed by analysts following the war that, by 1985, the Iraqis were unbeatable and that Iran was slowly being ground down and would probably lose.

79. It was not until October 2003 that the CIA admitted on its Web site in a report on Iraq's weapons of mass destruction that Iraq had not used gas in the final campaign against Iran in 1988.

80. For an insightful (and often amusing) treatment of this national character trait see Thorstein Veblen's *Absentee Ownership* (New York: Augustus Kelley, 1964), and *The Theory of Business Enterprise* (New Brunswick, N.J.: Transactions Publishers, 1996).

81. Actually there was Casper Weinberger, who often seemed a lot more competent along those lines than George Shultz.

82. "U.S. Welcomes Move by Tehran," *New York Times*, July 17, 1988.

83. "U.S. Charges Iraq used Gas on Kurds," *Washington Post*, September 9, 1988.

84. "Iraq Denies Using Chemical Weapons on Kurds," *Washington Post*, September 16, 1988.

85. The charges are contained in the staffers report, *Chemical Weapons Use in Kurdistan: Iraq's Final Offensive*, September 21, 1988.

86. The U.S. Army War College published a study in which it examined the claim of the Iraqis' use of chemicals against the Kurds Halabja. Based on an investigation by the U.S. Defense Intelligence Agency, it found that it was Iranian gas—not Iraqi—that killed the Kurds, and in the process of making that assertion, it rebutted the staff report, pointing out the claim of so many deaths in a compressed time period was impossible. See *Lessons Learned: the Iran-Iraq War* (Carlisle, Pa.: Strategic Studies Institute, 1991).

87. "Stopping Saddam's Drive for Dominance," *Washington Post Outlook*, August 5, 1990; "Iraq's Criminal Credit Line," *New York Times*, October 26, 1989; "Israeli Defenses against Arab Gas-Attacks, *Manchester Guardian*, March 12, 1989; "Iraq Said Developing A-Weapons," *Washington Post*, March 31, 1989; "The Middle East's Awful Arms Race: Greater Threats from Lesser Powers," *New York Times*, April 8, 1990; "Iraq's Arsenal of Horrors," *Washington Post*, April 8, 1990; "Why Are We Helping the Third World Go Nueclear?" *Washington Post Outlook*, April 1990; "Arab Weapons Challenge Israel's Role in the Region," *Washington Post*, April 4, 1990; "Iraq Said to Build Launchers for 400-mile Missile," *New York Times*, March 30, 1990; "To Combat the Growing Iraqi Threat," *New York Times*, May 30, 1990; "Israel Looks Around and Finds New Causes to Worry," *New York Times*, May 27, 1990; "Turning a Blind Eye to Baghdad," *Washington Post*, July 5, 1990; "Must the U.S. Give Brazil and Iraq the Bomb?" *New York Times*, July 30, 1990.

88. And, of course, the Iraqis could not build an A-bomb, as the Israelis had destroyed their only nuclear reactor in 1981 and it had never been rebuilt.

89. That is the way the Saudis understood the case; they never asked for repayment.

90. The sheikhdom had gotten itself involved in two nasty scandals. In one, Kuwaitis were rigging the bourse. The government absorbed the losses of its malfeasant citizens. In the other, the sheikhdom lost heavily on bad investments in Spain.

91. This was brought out in the famous April Glaspie interview.

92. Iraq claimed that for every dollar the price of oil sank, Iraq lost a billion dollars in revenue.

93. Bush supported the visit of a Senate delegation to Baghdad to reassure the Iraqis of America's good intentions.

94. The CIA had been assuring the administration that Iraq could not possibly mobilize to take over Kuwait in anything less than two-weeks.

95. Saddam announced just before the war broke out that he intended to discipline OPEC; that is, make its members (chiefly the lesser sheikhdoms) stop cheating on their quotas. Had he been able to assume this role, he would have become the enforcer of an effective cartel, the role Britain fulfilled until 1973.

96. Small countries, such as the UAE and Kuwait, which have large reserves of oil and up-to-date facilities, which allow them to achieve high-volume production, can make money even when the price is low.

97. "OPEC Meets Today: Talks Are Clouded by Iraq's Threat to Kuwait," *New York Times*, July 25, 1990.

98. For example, Senator Alphonse D'Amato (R-NY), Senator Claiborne Pell (D-R), and Representative Howard Berman (D-CA).

Chapter 4

1. Schwartzkopf's original battle plan was an off-the-shelf version of a CENTCOM plan to block a Soviet invasion of Iran.

2. Iraq had a formidable military, by Middle East standards, but that was nothing against the power of the United States.

3. A coalition that eventually comprised twenty-eight nations.

4. Quoted in Dilip Hiro, *Desert Storm to Desert Shield* (New York: Routledge, 1992), 183.

5. *The St. Petersburg Times* of St. Petersburg, Fla. bought satellite pictures from the Russians that showed that the Iraqi force in Kuwait was one-fifth that claimed by the U.S. Defense Department. *Desert Shield to Desert Storm*, 121.

6. According to Hiro, such a letter was sent, in which Saddam asked—in return for his withdrawal from Kuwaiti—for the retention of Bubiyan and Warbah and an area of northern Kuwait bordering Iraq, plus the

cancellation of Iraq's wartime debts to both the West and the Arab States; *Desert Shield to Desert Storm*, 118.

7. Said Aburish, *Saddam Hussein: The Politics of Revenge*, 286.

8. Dilip Hiro, *Desert Shield to Desert Storm*, 119.

9. Dilip Hiro mentions the majority vote aspect of the Arab League meeting, but he does not discuss the role of Mubarak and Fahd in overturning League rules; Ibid., 122.

10. Although on balance, considering the trading privileges with the Iraqis and the transit fees for transporting Iraqi oil through Turkish territory, all of which were lost, the Turks ultimately did very badly.

11. Dilip Hiro, *Desert Shield to Desert Storm*, 125.

12. Syria got $2.2 billion from the Saudis and Kuwaitis.

13. Dilip Hiro, *Desert Shield to Desert Storm*, 130.

14. Interestingly, the largest demonstrations, from the very first, were in the countries of the Magreb, and particularly Algeria, which confounded the terror theorists who claimed that the Islamic Fundamentalist movement was being directed by the Gulf sheikhs. The eruptions in Algiers horrified the Saudis and Kuwaitis and in response the sheikhs withdrew their support for the Islamic Salvation Front.

15. Clayton Newell, *Historical Dictionary of the Persian Gulf War: 1990–1991* (Lanham, Md.: Scarecrow Press, 1998).

16. Dilip Hiro, *Desert Shield to Desert Storm*, 148.

17. Clayton Newell, *Historical Dictionary of the Persian Gulf War*, 9.

18. Ibid., 205.

19. One has the feeling this was Mubarak's course of action.

20. Dilip Hiro, *Desert Shield to Desert Storm*, 108.

21. Dilip Hiro, *The Longest War* (New York: Routledge, 1991), 230.

22. The demonizing started when Bush accused Saddam of gassing his own people, citing Halabja. Only months before, his administration had absolved Saddam from complicity in that affair. See the author's "War Crime or Act of War," *New York Times*, January 31, 2003.

23. Dilip Hiro, *Desert Shield to Desert Storm*, 229.

24. The best information on the Republican Guard appears in the author's book, *The Iran-Iraq War: Chaos in a Vacuum*, and in Stephen Pelletière, Douglas Johnson, and Lief Rosenberger, *Iraqi Power and U.S. Security in the Middle East* (Carlisle, Pa.: The Strategic Studies Institute, 1990), and in *Lessons Learned: the Iran-Iraq War* (Carlisle, Pa.: The Strategic Studies Institute, 1991).

25. For a discussion of the origins of air land battle, see Clayton Newell, *The Historical Dictionary of the Persian Gulf War*.

26. Based on discussions with knowledgeable officers in the Pentagon.

27. What one must assume is that, putting it this way (that they were going to go after Saddam and his entourage) was a euphemism; in fact what they were planning to hit were Iraqi cities, but they did not want to say that.

28. Ibid.

29. Ibid.

30. See Clayton Newell, *Historical Dictionary of the Persian Gulf War.*

31. Casualty figures are difficult to cite; the range is wide. The figure of Iraqi dead climbs as high as 100,000 (the estimate of the U.S. Defense Intelligence Agency), to a low of 10,000 (the U.S. Air Force estimate). Clearly, there are ideological considerations bound up in the various differing tallies.

32. "If Mid-East War Erupts Air Power Will Hold Key to U.S. Casualties," *Wall Street Journal*, November 15, 1990.

33. Dilip Hiro, *Desert Shield to Desert Storm*, 187–89.

34. "Studies: 70,000 Deaths in Postwar Iraq," *Phildelphia Inquirer*, January 9, 1992.

35. Dilip Hiro, *Desert Shield to Desert Storm*, 353.

36. Ibid., 350.

37. Ibid., 353–54.

38. The publishers agreed to embedding; that is, reporters were assigned to units and remained with them throughout the war. Nothing could have been better designed to achieve self-censorship than this.

39. Dilip Hiro, *Desert Shield to Desert Storm*, 346.

40. Ibid., 359.

41. Ibid.

42. For an account of the McCaffrey affair, see Seymour Hersh, "Overwhelming Force," *The New Yorker*, May 22, 2000.

43. "Report on Child Deaths in Iraq," *Al Quds al'Arabi* (London), June 24, 1999.

44. The Ba'thists had been singularly successfully in mobilizing for the Iran-Iraq War, putting together a million-man army. Since the population of the country was only about 12 million, this was phenomenal.

45. Dilip Hiro, *Desert Shield to Desert Storm*, 362.

46. Dilip Hiro says the bombs only accounted for 7 percent of explosives used in the war and that their accuracy was put at 60 percent; ibid., 332.

47. Indyk was executive director of the Washington Institute for Near East Policy Study, an AIPAC think-tank. He was also not an American but an

Australian citizen and had to be naturalized before he could go to work for the administration.

48. Peter Odell, professor emeritus of international energy studies at Erasmus University, Rotterdam, made these points at a forum on "Middle East Petroleum and UN/US Sanctions," held in Niciosia in 1997.

49. For example, they could not get chlorine to purify water because that was alleged to have a military application.

50. Denis J. Halliday, "The Impact of the UN Sanctions on the People of Iraq," *Journal of Palestine Studies* XXVIII (Winter 1999): 29–37. Halliday, who was assistant secretary general of the United Nations, resigned at the end of October 1998 from his post as UN Humanitarian Coordinator for the Oil-for-Food Program in protest against the way the sanctions were being manipulated by the United States and Britain.

51. Albright made the declaration to Lesley Stahl on CBS in 1996. See "How Sanctions Kill 4,000 Iraqi Kids a Month: Albright's Tiny Coffins," *CounterPunch*, September 16–30, 1999; "Alif Ba' Notes High Child Mortality Rate, *FBIS*, JN3011155499 Baghdad *Alif Ba'*, November 17, 1999, and Asad Bakir, *AAUG Monitor*, Spring 2000; "Iraq the Tragedy of Disease, Deformity and Death," and "Child Mortality Rose in Iraq," *Washington Post*, September 24, 1992.

52. The Iraqis insisted on firing at the Allied patrols because, as they correctly assessed, these were violations of Iraqi sovereignty.

53. "Saudis May Back Out of Billions Worth of Wartime Weapons Buys," *Aerospace Daily*, July 14, 1992. The first indication of trouble came in a story in the *Washington Post*, detailing what the paper called Saudi Arabia's "severe financial crunch." It was brought out that among its obligations were $6 billion in loan commitments, including $1.5 billion to the Soviet Union, plus payments to the following: $1.7 billion to Egypt; $1.2 billion to Turkey; $1.1 billion to $1.6 billion to Syria, and lesser amounts to Morocco, Lebanon, Somalia, Bahrain, and Djibouti. "Saudis Said to Owe $64 billion, Scrape to Meet Obligations," April 3, 1992.

54. Conversations with knowledgeable officials in the Pentagon.

55. "Bentson to Meet Saudi Ruler," *Washington Post*, September 23, 1994.

56. "Weapons Merchants Are Going Great Guns in Post-Cold War Era," *Wall Street Journal*, January 28, 1994.

57. The Saudis made difficulty in yet another area: they refused to maintain the equipment they bought from the Americans, nor would they train on it, taking the position they were merely warehousing the arms against the day when the Americans might use them. This was awkward, as it implied the Americans were mercenaries.

58. "Saudi Arabia, Its Purse Thinner, Learns How to Say 'No' to U.S.," *New York Times*, November 4, 1994. The author first learned of the Saudis' difficulties when he went out to the Gulf right after the first Gulf War. He did not believe it, so engrained was the notion of the Saudis being eternally well set up.

59. "Saudi Deals in 90's Shifting Away from Cash Toward Credit," *New York Times*, August 23, 1993.

60. Conversations with knowledgeable officials in the Pentagon. Also see "Saudi Arabia, Its Purse Thinner, Learns How to Say 'No' to U.S." The *Journal* story says the Saudis accused the Americans of overcharging them on the purchases.

61. "U.S.-Saudi Agreement is Reached on $9.2 Billion Arms Purchase Stretchout," *Washington Post*, February 1, 1994.

62. "Saudi Air to Buy $6 Billion in Jets Built in the U.S., *New York Times*, February 17, 1994.

63. This was truly ironic. The EX-IM arrangement is supposed to help poor Third World countries; the Saudis were hardly that.

64. "Saudis Set to Reduce Weapons Purchases," *Financial Times*, February 25, 1999.

65. "OPEC is Poised to Cut Output, Lift Oil Prices," *New York Times*, March 22, 1999; "The Saudi Oil Sector Confronts Reality," *Middle East International*, November 13, 1998.

66. "Cash Short Venezuela Turns to Foreign Oil Companies," *New York Times*, March 1996.

67. "Saudis Weigh U.S. Firms' Aid on Energy," *Washington Post*, February 6, 1999; Typical of the Iraqi criticism: "Article Criticizes Saudi Anti-Arab Stances," *FBIS*, FTS19981229000715; *Al Qds al-'Arabi* (London), December 28, 1999.

68. "With Oil Cuts, Why Invite Outsiders?" *New York Times*, March 30, 1999. Chavez' second move, or close to it, was to pay a personal call on Saddam Husayn, which sent jitters through the oil market.

69. "OPEC is Poised to Cut Output, Lift Oil Prices," *New York Times*, March 23, 1999.

70. "Consumers Hit as Fuel Prices Climb Sharply," *New York Times*, January 3, 2000.

71. "Oil's Pressure Points," *New York Times*, April 13, 2003.

72. "U.S. Oil Output Drops, Consumption also Falls," *New York Times*, November 16, 1992; "Oil Activity Shifts from U.S.," *New York Times*, July 2, 1990.

73. "Deficit Soared in U.S. During July," *New York Times*, September 19, 1996.

74. "U.S. Troops Settle in the Arabian Desert," *Washington Post*, May 3, 2001. The Americans finally pulled out of Prince Sultan Air Base on August 28, 2003, leaving a skeleton crew at a remote desert facility.

75. This was the Barak plan whereby Barak, the Israeli prime minister, and Arafat were supposedly to come to a compromise, which would secure peace. In fact, the Arabs' eyes, the plan constituted a sell-out of the Palestinians by the Clinton administration.

76. "Greater Reliance on Foreign Oil Feared as U.S. Output Tumbles," *New York Times*, January 18, 1990.

77. "America's Oil Change," *New York Times*, October 30, 1997. Also, "Imports of Oil by U.S. Jumped 9.2% in 6 Months," *New York Times*, July 15, 1993.

78. The Israelis are inimical to the Sudanese because they are Arab. The Egyptians have long been hostile, a situation that dates back to the last century. Sudan was once part of Egypt and was broken away during the British occupation. The Egyptians want it back.

Chapter 5

1. To be sure, there was also North Korea, and the Pentagon could have worked up a crisis at any time over Taiwan, but, as assets, these were not as valuable as was the Gulf. It being part of the Middle East, the Israelis were heavily involved with its affairs. Having a homegrown constituency of American-Jews, who would turn out in support of an often-beleaguered Pentagon, was helpful, but even more the military could use AIPAC, one of the best organized lobbies in the United States. See "Divide Among Jews Leads to Silence on Iraq War," *New York Times*, March 15, 2003; "Some of Intellectual Left's Longtime Doves Taking on Role of Hawks," *New York Times*, March 14, 2003.

2. Don M. Snider, "The Coming Defense Train Wreck. . . ." *The Washington Quarterly* (Winter 1996).

3. This interpretation requires that chemical weapons be considered weapons of mass destruction, which, as we said above, they are not.

4. "9/11 Panel Issues Subpoena to Pentagon, Citing Delays," *New York Times*, November 8, 2002.

5. "Israel Winning Broad Support from U.S. Right," *New York Times*, April 21, 2002.

6. "Islam Is Violent, Pat Robertson Says," *New York Times*, February 23, 2002.

7. The architect of U.S. air operations during the 1991 Gulf War was John Warden. See "Airborne Ferocity Is the Best Strategy," *Financial Times*, March 18, 2003.

8. Interestingly, this is the same argument the Germans used to sell the blitzkrieg concept of warfare: that it was economical. See Gordon Wright, *The Ordeal of Total War: 1939–1945* (New York: Harper & Row, 1968), 44–52.

9. The board comprises senior statesmen who supposedly advise on defense policy, but who almost assuredly also lobby for the department. It is not an official government body but meets informally. Richard Perle, the leading neo-con, was until recently the head of the board, a post he was forced to relinquish after a conflict of interest scandal. See appendix B.

10. " 'We now have the armaments to accomplish in 24 or 36 hours what took seven days in 1991,' " *Financial Times*, March 20, 2003.

11. Ibid.

12. Ibid.

13. "U.S Bombs Aid Rebels in North; Propaganda Campaign Intensified," *Washington Post*, November 8, 2001; "Afghan Rebels Close in on Pivotal City," *Washington Post*, November 2001; and "Ruined Fortress Is Strewn with Taliban Corpses," *Washington Post*," November 29, 2001.

14. "War Widens Ethnic Divide," *Washington Post*, November 9, 2001.

15. "Deal-Making Let Many Leaders of Taliban Escape," *Washington Post*, December 17, 2001.

16. The Hazaras are the Shias the Iranians befriended that provoked the intervention by the CIA against the Russians.

17. "Al Qaeda's Forces Flee Caves for Mountains," *Washington Post*, December 11, 2003; "Afghans' Retreat Forced Americans to Lead a Battle," *New York Times*, March 10, 2002.

18. "U.S. Putting Off Plan to Use G.I.'s in Afghan Caves," *New York Times*, December 27, 2001.

19. "Bravery and Breakdowns in a Ridgetop Battle," *Washington Post*, May 24, 2002; and "Seven U.S. Soldiers Die in Battle," *Washington Post*, March 5, 2002.

20. "CIA's Cash Toppled Taliban," *Washington Post*, November 16, 2002.

21. "Qaeda Survivors by the Hundreds Said to Disappear," *New York Times*, December 19, 2001.

22. Conversations with knowledgeable parties in the Pentagon.

23. " 'It's the same,' " *Patriot News* (Harrisburg, Pa.), April 22, 2002.

24. "Behind Confident Front, Karzai's Control Often Illusory," *Washington Post*, February 25, 2002.

25. "Afghanistan Opium Crop Threatens Europe," *Financial Times*, February 18, 2002; "Afghan Poppy Farmers Resist Attempts to Destroy Crop," *Financial Times*, April 10, 2002.

26. "Refugees Start Returning Home," *Washington Post*, December 15, 2001; "Afghans Return to Start Over," *Washington Post*, March 21, 2002.

27. Ibid.

28. "Resurgent Taliban Threatens Afghan Stability, U.S. Says," *New York Times*, November 19, 2003; "Along Afghan Border, Pakistan Finds It Hard to Assert Control, *New York Times*, June 3, 2002.

29. Bush at one point said that the Iraqis could do this, and when it was pointed out to him they had no missile capable of reaching U.S. shores, he said they could launch from a ship in the Atlantic Ocean!

30. "Rumsfeld Turns Eye to Future of Army," *Washington Post*, June 8, 2003.

31. "No One Is Laughing at Iraq's Exiles Now," *New York Times, Week In Review*, May 11, 2003.

32. "Blair Says Iraqis Could Launch Chemical Warheads in Minutes," *New York Times*, September 25, 2002; "Britain Outlines 'Overwhelming' Case against Iraq," *Financial Times*, September 25, 2002.

33. "Pentagon and Bogus News: All Is Denied," *New York Times*," December 5, 2003; "Frustrated U.S. Arms Team to Leave Iraq," *Washington Post*, May 11, 2003.

34. "Mr. Murdoch's War," *New York Times*, April 7, 2003.

35. "US Lobbyists Seek to Cash in on Rush for Reconstruction Work," *Financial Times*, November 12, 2003.

36. "Military Sales Help Lift Boeing's Quarterly Profit," *New York Times*, October 30, 2003.

37. "Conservative Republicans Push For Slowdown in U.S. Spending," *New York Times*, January 22, 2004.

38. Of course Cheney is the former CEO of Halliburton; Shultz of Bechtel. "Evidence Is Cited of Overcharging in Iraq Contract," *New York Times*," December 12, 2003; High Payments to Halliburton for Fuel in Iraq," *New York Times*, December 10, 2003; "At U.S. Meeting, Iraq Appears Open for Business," *New York Times*, December 5, 2003.

39. Perle particularly seems to have benefited from the wars. He has a private consulting firm, which recently has exposed him to several conflict of interest allegations. See "A Cosy Relationship: Boeing's Pentagon Deal Bears Testament to Its Skilful Lobbying Efforts," *Financial Times*, Februrary 8, 2003; "Misinformation at Heart of Hollinger Payout," *Financial Times*, December 5, 2003; "Report Finds No Violations at Pentagon by Advisor," *New York Times*, November 15, 2003; "SEC Issues Subpoenas to Hollinger Officials," *New York Times*, November 20, 2003; "Uncertified Results Filed by Publisher," *New York Times*, December 22, 2003; "Perle Threatens Lawsuit over Hersh Article in *New Yorker*," *Washington Post*, March 4,

2003; "Advisor to U.S. Aided Maker of Satellites," *New York Times*, March 29, 2003.

40. Boykin is an air force general who subsequently was involved with torture of Iraqis at the infamous Abu Ghrayb Prison.

41. One reaction to this was the convening of the so-called Tri-Lateral Commission in 1975, which specifically dealt with the problem of over-population.

42. As evidence of this, there was a movement, seemingly strong, at this time to have Japan and Germany become members of the Security Council.

43. "U.S. Strategy Calls for Insuring no Rivals Develop," *New York Times*, March 8, 1992; "Senior U.S. Officials Assail Lone-Superpower Policy," *New York Times*, March 11, 1992.

44. The directive was so offensive to America's allies that Bush was forced to repudiate it.

45. It is not widely recognized, but Iraq, in addition to having what may be the world's largest reserves of oil, also has the Middle East's most extensive water supplies. See the author's "War Crime, or Act of War," *New York Times*, January 31, 2003.

46. "Military Study Mulled Deterrence of 'Fear'," *Washington Post*, July 5, 2001.

47. Of interest is that Chavez, as soon as he took office, made a special trip to Iraq to meet with Saddam. This particularly angered the Americans. But we feel it bolsters our theory that the high absorbers were maneuvering to take control of OPEC.

Index

About the Author

Stephen Pelletière was the Central Intelligence Agency's senior political analyst on Iraq during the Iran-Iraq War. From 1988 to 2000 he was a professor of National Security Affairs at the U.S. Army War College, Carlisle, Pa. Dr. Pelletière got his Ph.D. in Political Science from the University of California, Berkeley. He studied Arabic at the American University in Egypt and did his Ph.D. research at the Dar al Kutb in Cairo. He has published three other books on Iraq, two for Praeger: *The Iran-Iraq War: Chaos in a Vacuum*, 1992, and *Iraq and the International Oil System—Why America Went to War in the Gulf*, 2000.